Democracy Under Construction

A Reader by Wyoming Humanities

Democracy Under Construction

A Reader by Wyoming Humanities

Edited by Dr. Scott Henkel
Director, Wyoming Institute for
Humanities Research
Board of Directors, Wyoming Humanities

Dr. Scott Henkel, Editor-in-Chief
Dr. Erin Pryor Ackerman, Co-Editor
Josh Watanabe, Co-Editor

First printing, 2020
Printed in the United States of America

LIBRARY OF CONGRESS METADATA
Civil Disobedience in Literature
Civil Disobedience—United States
Democracy
Democracy in literature
Democracy—History
Democracy—United States
Humanities
Humanities literature
Humanities—History
Indians of North America
Indians of North America—Culture
Race Discrimination—United States
Social Movements
Social Movements—United States
Social Movements in Literature
United States—Race Relations
Women—Suffrage—United States
Wyoming
Wyoming—History

Cover: Photo by Wyoming Capital Square Project, 2018
Printed by Mondo Solutions

Contents

Contents

Editor's Introduction

democracy

noun de·moc·ra·cy \di-'mä-krə-sē\

From ancient Greek: δημοκρατία "popular government"; combination of δῆμος (demos), meaning the commons, the people + -κρατια (kratos), meaning power, rule, or authority

1: government by the people: majority rule
2: government in which the highest power is held by the people and is usually used through representatives
3: a political unit (as a nation) governed by the people
4: belief in or practice of the idea that all people are socially equal

I want you to think about a big idea. It's this: you can shape your community, your nation, and the world in which you live. In a democracy, the people have power; that means if you're a person, you have some power.

The exciting and also hard part about this is everyone can be a part of the democratic process. Our democracy hasn't always lived up to that ideal, but if that process is working well, we have to figure out ways to make our communities thrive, together. That's a challenge, but it's one part of what it means to live in a democracy. Another part of what democracy means is that it's always changing.

When we were putting this book together, our state capitol in Cheyenne was under renovation and construction. I love that the cover of this book has a picture of our state capitol at that moment. It is a perfect metaphor for democracy: we are always under construction. We have a history, and we have a future. It is up to us to learn that history and to shape our future. What could our democracy look like? People often think about democracy as a form of government, and that's perfectly reasonable. But as the definition suggests, democracy is also a type of power. These two interpretations, democracy as a form of government and democracy as a type of power, are what I hope you think about as you read the essays in this volume.

The first interpretation—democracy as a form of government—is what President Lincoln meant when he hoped, in the last line of the Gettysburg Address, that a "government of the people, by the people, and for the people shall not perish from the earth." The second interpretation—democracy as a type of power—may be a bit less familiar, but it's hidden in plain sight, and once you see it, you'll know it.

That second interpretation of democracy helps us all to feel our value and why we are important and helps us understand better where we've come from and where we might be going. There is a power—a democratic power that is part of every one of us—when we think in creative and critical ways. Let me repeat that: the power to think creatively and critically is in every single one of us. It is not something that only a few, special people possess. We have the potential to think, to act, and to do so in a way that helps our communities be vibrant.

Helping us to see this democratic power is one of the roles the humanities play in our world. The humanities are the study of the human experience. What does it mean to be human? How do we live, what have we been, what could we become? How should we express ourselves in our communities? How should we interact with our beautiful Wyoming natural world? In schools and at the University of Wyoming, these questions get asked in research and classes in *American Studies; History; Literature; Languages; Philosophy; Religious Studies; Cultural Studies; Critical Race, Class, and Gender Studies; Law;* and more. The humanities speak to our most profound needs, like a commitment to ethics, discovery, and critical thinking. Listening to the stories we tell helps us understand who we are and who we could be.

The problem, of course, is that the world we live in is not always just and fair. Sometimes our world can be a difficult place, with problems that must be addressed if we are to live up to our highest ideals of democracy, freedom, and justice.

We have much to be proud of in Wyoming. As T. A. Larson documents in his *History of Wyoming*, after Wyoming became the first state to legally recognize a woman's right to vote, Susan B. Anthony said, during a visit to Laramie, "Wyoming is the only place on God's green earth which could consistently claim to be the land of the free!" But we also have a good ways yet to go.

For those reasons and more, we have put together this book. It includes some of the most critical and creative thinking in our history and our present. The authors here took on some of the difficult issues of their day, which are sometimes still issues we deal with in our time.

As you read these pieces, you might ask yourself:

- How free is your speech? Does it take courage to speak? Are there some ideas that should not be a part of a civil community?
- What is the value of political debate? Does it help us understand the truth?
- How should we understand civility? How should we understand protest in a free community?
- Even though many of these readings are from different eras, how can they help us understand our time?
- How can we use these ideas to solve the problems that will come up in our communities?
- What will our future look like, and what role will we play in it?

What could our democracy be?

The pieces in this book bring a diverse set of experiences and viewpoints to that question. These authors do not always agree with one another. Yet that diversity, that exchange of ideas is part of what makes our world a rich one. We invite you to enter this conversation, too—if democracy is always under construction, what do you think it could it look like in ten or a hundred years?

Dr. Scott Henkel
Director, Wyoming Institute for Humanities Research
Board of Directors, Wyoming Humanities

Introduction from the Executive Director

Democracy Under Construction demonstrates Wyoming Humanities' unique ability to bring together a network of individuals and organizations to complete a project that helps our state explore the human experience. Like all of our work, this publication is the result of extensive collaboration—from a wide and diverse array of funders to the myriad scholars, experts, and authors who provided generous gifts of time, intellect, and writing.

This book was conceived as a second volume to our popular *Heal Up and Hair Over: A Wyoming Civility Reader,* which was distributed from 2013 to 2018. This new volume was partially funded by a grant from The Andrew W. Mellon Foundation for the "Democracy and the Informed Citizen" initiative to which every state council could apply for funds to support projects that examine the connections between democracy, the humanities, journalism, and an informed citizenry. As part of our project in Wyoming, we explored the issue of civility in journalism and social media and how it is eroding the public trust in the institutions of democracy.

Incivility, we determined, is not necessarily the cause of America's growing distrust, it is a symptom. Taking to task examples of civil versus uncivil behavior and dissecting the difference between civil disobedience and incivility is an important part of any conversation about the state of our democracy. We include here examinations of civility and its role in the democratic process as part of a more wide-ranging collection that we hope promotes conversations about the state of American democracy by taking a deep dive into the intent and expression of democracy as our nation's form of government and the concept of democracy as a type of inherent power that individuals possesses.

Some of our state's most well-known historians and thinkers graciously granted permission to republish their powerful commentary and analysis. A few contributors wrote new content for us. Please take a moment to read the biographies of our authors—it's a true who's who of thoughtful, provocative, and evocative writers in Wyoming and beyond. We are deeply grateful for their contributions.

The project editor, Dr. Scott Henkel, Director of the Wyoming Institute for Humanities Research at the University of Wyoming and Associate Professor of English and African American and Diaspora Studies, with a specialty in democratic political movements and free speech and censorship, led us in the production of the book.

The staff of Wyoming Humanities worked closely with Dr. Henkel to manage the creation of this publication. Josh Watanabe, Erin Pryor Ackerman, Sheila Bricher-Wade, and Emy diGrappa all played a role in defining the scope, acquiring content and permissions, designing the cover, and handling the printing logistics. Our marketing agency, Mondo Solutions, handled the graphic design, book layout, and copy-editing.

In addition to funding provided by The Andrew W. Mellon Foundation through the Federation of State Humanities Councils, funding for this book was provided through the National Endowment for the Humanities, and the Wyoming Department of State Parks and Cultural Resources through funding approved by the Wyoming State Legislature. We gratefully acknowledge this partnership and the cooperative work with Wyoming State Parks and Cultural Resources Director Darin Westby and staff as well as the leadership from former Governor Matt Mead and current Governor Mark Gordon and the many legislative leaders whose support ensures our work serves the entire state.

As a nonprofit, we are managed by a board of directors

who are passionate about the humanities and their ability to help Wyomingites understand our history, engage with tough topics today, and shape a better tomorrow. These people are devoted to making a better Wyoming, and I am honored to serve at their pleasure.

Shannon D. Smith
Executive Director and CEO, Wyoming Humanities

About Wyoming Humanities

Wyoming Humanities is a 501c3 independent nonprofit corporation and Wyoming's affiliate of the National Endowment for the Humanities (NEH). We are one of 56 state and jurisdictional humanities councils and have promoted the public humanities in Wyoming through grants and programs since 1970. Our funding comes from the NEH and the State of Wyoming, as well as private sources including foundation grants, corporate sponsorships, and individual donations.

Our purpose is to use the humanities to strengthen our democracy, expand the Wyoming narrative, and promote engaged communities. We are a statewide organization that strives to serve all 23 counties and 99 communities of Wyoming every year. Find out more about us at *www.thinkwy.org.*

Wyoming Humanities Board of Directors (2020)

Rev. Dr. Bernadine Craft, Rock Springs, *Chair*
Milward Simpson, Cheyenne, *Chair-Elect*
Carol Seeger, Gillette, *Past Chair*
Mary B. Guthrie, Cheyenne
Hon. Nancy J. Guthrie, Jackson
Willie LeClair, Riverton
Barbara McNab, Big Horn
Dr. Maggi Maier Murdock, Casper/Laramie
Rev. Warren Murphy, Cody
Fred Schmechel, Laramie
Sarah Jo Sinclair, Sheridan
Kristi Wallin, Cheyenne
Isabel Zumel, Jackson
Dr. Sandra Caldwell, Cheyenne, *Ex Officio, Wyoming Community College Commission*
Dr. Scott Henkel, Laramie, *Ex Officio, Wyoming Institute for Humanities Research*

Wyoming Humanities Staff (2020)

Shannon D. Smith, Laramie, *Executive Director and CEO*
Shawn Reese, Laramie, *Chief Operating Officer*
Josh Watanabe, Laramie, *Director of Operations*
Erin Pryor Ackerman, Laramie, *Director of Grants and Community Engagement*
Mark Jenkins, Laramie, *Resident Scholar*
Emy diGrappa, Jackson, *Executive Producer*

Historical Context

Teena Gabrielson

Born and raised in Minnesota, Teena received an undergraduate degree from Macalester College before moving to Northern California to earn a Ph.D. in Political Science from the University of California, Davis. Despite spring, or late winter, Teena loves Wyoming weather. She arrived in Wyoming 2006 as a professor in the Department of Political Science, now the School of Politics, Public Affairs, and International Studies. Teena is trained as a political theorist and researches within the field of environmental political theory focusing on questions of environmental justice.

After serving as Department Head from 2014 to 2017, she became Associate Dean in 2017 in which capacity she oversees the departments of English, Geography, Modern and Classical Languages, Philosophy and Religious Studies, the School of Culture, Gender and Social Justice, Theatre and Dance, and Zoology and Physiology. Teena also serves as the liaison to the Office of Diversity, Equity, and Inclusion.

Introduction

In 2017, on the cusp of the 230th anniversary of the Constitutional Convention, the University of Pennsylvania's Annenberg Public Policy Center released survey data showing that 37% of American respondents could not name any of the five rights protected by the First Amendment and only 48% could name freedom of speech. This statistic is alarming because democratic governance depends upon the ability of citizens to gather information and opinions, to deliberate, and to peacefully protest. The selection of readings collected here probe both the value of speech to citizenship and the problems that arise with free speech in representative democracies. In October 1788, James Madison shared his thoughts on the Bill of Rights in a letter to his longtime friend Thomas Jefferson. Among his concerns was a fear that the Bill of Rights would merely serve as a "parchment barrier" to power, insufficient to thwart the will of a majority. Madison explained that for the Bill of Rights to become a powerful tool, its measures must be "incorporated with the national sentiment," such that most Americans would understand its advantages and jealously guard the rights and liberties it articulated. In his essay "Public Opinion," Madison restates this position in more general terms, claiming that public opinion "sets the bounds to every government." In helping us to see the importance of public opinion to the protection of individual rights, Madison's work further underscores what the statistic above makes apparent—civic education is critical to the protection of liberty.

The readings in this section develop a variety of lines of thought, many of which emerge in contemporary debates. For instance, both Ralph Waldo Emerson and Elizabeth Cady Stanton point to the relationships between free speech, freedom of conscience, and the development of personal identity. To speak freely, particularly when advancing an unpopular position, requires courage. In his frank assessment, Alexis de Tocqueville observes that there is no other country with less "independence of mind and true freedom of discussion than in America" due to the tyranny of the majority and the security that conformity provides. Emphasizing the importance of deliberation to the protection of liberty in representative democracies, John Stuart Mill highlights the silencing effect of vituperative speech while Frederick Douglass convincingly demonstrates that there is a time for "biting ridicule, blasting reproach, withering sarcasm, and stern rebuke." While differing in intention and tone, Tecumseh, Sojourner Truth, Susan B. Anthony, and Henry David Thoreau all use speech to protest existing policy and to reveal the ways that speech can be used to both create community and to exclude, isolate, and marginalize. Abraham Lincoln's brief Second Inaugural begins the work of suturing a nation rent by war. We hope that the individual readings in this section can be brought into productive tension with each other to promote discussion on the role of deliberation, free speech, civility, protest, and public opinion in democratic practice and governance.

Alexis de Tocqueville

July 29, 1805 – April 16, 1859

Alexis de Tocqueville was a French diplomat, historian, and political scientist. He was very active on the French politcal stage and was a classical liberal whose politics tended to be just left of center. He believed in democracy over monachy and advocated for a parliamentary government. He is best known for his books *Democracy in America* and *The Old Regime and the Revolution*. *Democracy in America* is still celebrated as an early work of sociology and political science; it examines the ever-improving social conditions in America and explores why a representative democracy was successfully established in America but struggled to take hold in other countries.

From Democracy in America, Vol II (1835)

It must be acknowledged that amongst few of the civilized nations of our time have the higher sciences made less progress than in the United States; and in few have great artists, fine poets, or celebrated writers been more rare. Many Europeans, struck by this fact, have looked upon it as a natural and inevitable result of equality; and they have supposed that if a democratic state of society and democratic institutions were ever to prevail over the whole earth, the human mind would gradually find its beacon-lights grow dim, and men would relapse into a period of darkness. To reason thus is, I think, to confound several ideas which it is important to divide and to examine separately: it is to mingle, unintentionally, what is democratic with what is only American. . . .

The Americans are a very old and a very enlightened people, who have fallen upon a new and unbounded country, where they may extend themselves at pleasure, and which they may fertilize without difficulty. This state of things is without a parallel in the history of the world. In America, then, every one finds facilities, unknown elsewhere, for making or increasing his fortune. The spirit of gain is always on the stretch, and the human mind, constantly diverted from the pleasures of imagination and the labors of the intellect, is there swayed by no impulse but the pursuit of wealth. Not only are manufacturing and commercial classes to be found in the United States, as they are in all other countries; but what never occurred elsewhere, the whole community is simultaneously engaged in productive industry and commerce. I am convinced that, if the Americans had been alone in the world, with the freedom and the knowledge acquired by their forefathers, and the passions which are their own, they would not have been slow to discover that progress cannot long be made in the application of the sciences without cultivating the theory of them; that all the arts are perfected by one another: and, however absorbed they might have been by the pursuit of the principal object of their desires, they would speedily have admitted, that it is necessary to turn aside from it occasionally, in order the better to attain it in the end. . . .

Not only will the number of those who can take an interest in the productions of the mind be enlarged, but the taste for intellectual enjoyment will descend, step by step, even to those who, in aristocratic societies, seem to have neither time nor ability to in indulge in them. When hereditary wealth, the privileges of rank, and the prerogatives of birth have ceased to be, and when every man derives his strength from himself alone, it becomes evident that the chief cause of disparity between the fortunes of men is the mind. Whatever tends to invigorate, to extend, or to adorn the mind, instantly rises to great value. The utility of knowledge becomes singularly conspicuous even to the eyes of the multitude: those who have no taste for its charms set store upon its results, and make some efforts to acquire it. In free and enlightened democratic ages, there is nothing to separate men from each other or to retain them in their peculiar sphere; they rise or sink with extreme rapidity. All classes live in perpetual intercourse from their great proximity to each other. They communicate and intermingle every day—they imitate and envy one other: this suggests to the people many ideas, notions, and desires which it would never have entertained if the distinctions of rank had been fixed and society at rest. In such nations the servant never considers himself as an entire stranger to the pleasures and toils of his master, nor the poor man to those of the rich; the rural population assimilates itself to that of the towns, and the provinces to the capital. No one easily allows himself to be reduced to the mere material cares of life; and the humblest artisan casts at times an eager and a furtive glance into the higher regions of the intellect. People do not read with the same notions or in the same manner as they do in an aristocratic community; but the circle of readers is unceasingly expanded, till it includes all the citizens.

As soon as the multitude begins to take an interest in the labors of the mind, it finds out that to excel in some of them is a powerful method of acquiring fame, power, or wealth. The restless ambition which equality begets instantly takes this direction as it does all others. The number of those who cultivate science, letters, and the arts, becomes immense. The intellectual world starts into prodigious activity: everyone endeavors to open for himself a path there, and to draw the eyes of the public after him. Something analogous occurs to what happens in society in the United States, politically considered. What is done is often imperfect, but the attempts are innumerable; and, although the results of individual effort are commonly very small, the total amount is always very large.

It is therefore not true to assert that men living in

democratic ages are naturally indifferent to science, literature, and the arts: only it must be acknowledged that they cultivate them after their own fashion, and bring to the task their own peculiar qualifications and deficiencies.

John Stuart Mill

May 20, 1806 – May 7, 1873

John Stuart Mill was a British civil servant, political economist, and philosopher. Mill made great contributions to social and political theory and to political economy. He was a proponent of classical liberalism—which calls for upholding civil liberties and emphasizes economic freedom—and utilitarianism. Utilitarianism advocates for the maximized happiness and well-being of the majority. Part of the Liberal Party and a member of Parliament, he supported women's suffrage. His support of gender equality is reflected in his book *The Subjugation of Women*, published in 1869. He also supported the abolition of slavery in the United States (it was abolished in England in 1833). Ultimately, Mill's conception of liberty placed the rights and freedom of the individual over state and social control.

From On Liberty (1859)

The object of this Essay is to assert one very simple principle, as entitled to govern absolutely the dealings of society with the individual in the way of compulsion and control, whether the means used be physical force in the form of legal penalties, or the moral coercion of public opinion. That principle is, that the sole end for which mankind are warranted, individually or collectively, in interfering with the liberty of action of any of their number, is self-protection. That the only purpose for which power can be rightfully exercised over any member of a civilised community, against his will, is to prevent harm to others. His own good, either physical or moral, is not a sufficient warrant. He cannot rightfully be compelled to do or forbear because it will be better for him to do so, because it will make him happier, because, in the opinions of others, to do so would be wise, or even right. These are good reasons for remonstrating with him, or reasoning with him, or persuading him, or entreating him, but not for compelling him, or visiting him with any evil in case he do otherwise. To justify that, the conduct from which it is desired to deter him must be calculated to produce evil to some one else. The only part of the conduct of any one, for which he is amenable to society, is that which concerns others. In the part which merely concerns himself, his independence is, of right, absolute. Over himself, over his own body and mind, the individual is sovereign. . . .

[T]he dictum that truth always triumphs over persecution, is one of those pleasant falsehoods which men repeat after one another till they pass into commonplaces, but which all experience refutes. History teems with instances of truth put down by persecution. If not suppressed for ever, it may be thrown back for centuries. To speak only of religious opinions: the Reformation broke out at least twenty times before Luther, and was put down. Arnold of Brescia was put down. Fra Dolcino was put down. Savonarola was put down. The Albigeois were put down. The Vaudois were put down. The Lollards were put down. The Hussites were put down. Even after the era of Luther, wherever persecution was persisted in, it was successful. In Spain, Italy, Flanders, the Austrian empire, Protestantism was rooted out; and, most likely, would have been so in England, had Queen Mary lived, or Queen Elizabeth died. Persecution has always succeeded, save where the heretics were too strong a party to be effectually persecuted. No reasonable person can doubt that Christianity might have been extirpated in the Roman Empire. It spread, and became predominant, because the persecutions were only occasional, lasting but a short time, and separated by long intervals of almost undisturbed propagandism. It is a piece of idle sentimentality that truth, merely as truth, has any inherent power denied to error, of prevailing against the dungeon and the stake. Men are not more zealous for truth than they often are for error, and a sufficient application of legal or even of social penalties will generally succeed in stopping the propagation of either. The real advantage which truth has, consists in this, that when an opinion is true, it may be extinguished once, twice, or many times, but in the course of ages there will generally be found persons to rediscover it, until some one of its reappearances falls on a time when from favourable circumstances it escapes persecution until it has made such head as to withstand all subsequent attempts to suppress it. . . .

For the interest, therefore, of truth and justice, it is far more important to restrain this employment of vituperative language than the other; and, for example, if it were necessary to choose, there would be much more need to discourage offensive attacks on infidelity, than on religion. It is, however, obvious that law and authority have no business with restraining either, while opinion ought, in every instance, to determine its verdict by the circumstances of the individual case; condemning every one, on whichever side of the argument he places himself, in whose mode of advocacy either want of candour, or malignity, bigotry, or intolerance of feeling manifest themselves; but not inferring these vices from the side which a person takes, though it be the contrary side of the question to our own: and giving merited honour to every one, whatever opinion he may hold, who has calmness to see and honesty to state what his opponents and their opinions really are, exaggerating nothing to their discredit, keeping nothing back which tells, or can be supposed to tell, in their favour. This is the real morality of public discussion; and if often violated, I am happy to think that there are many controversialists who to a great extent observe it, and a still greater number who conscientiously strive towards it.

Declaration of Independence of the United States

(1776)

When, in the Course of human events, it becomes necessary for one people to dissolve the political bands which have connected them with another, and to assume, among the powers of the earth, the separate and equal station to which the Laws of Nature and of Nature's God entitle them, a decent respect to the opinions of mankind requires that they should declare the causes which impel them to the separation.

We hold these truths to be self-evident, that all men are created equal, that they are endowed, by their Creator, with certain unalienable Rights, that among these are Life, Liberty, and the pursuit of Happiness. That to secure these rights, Governments are instituted among Men, deriving their just powers from the consent of the governed, That whenever any Form of Government becomes destructive of these ends, it is the Right of the People to alter or to abolish it, and to institute a new Government, laying its foundation on such principles and organizing its powers in such form as to them shall seem most likely to effect their Safety and Happiness. Prudence, indeed, will dictate, that Governments long established, should not be changed for light and transient causes; and accordingly all experience hath shewn, that mankind are more disposed to suffer, while evils are sufferable, than to right themselves by abolishing the forms to which they are accustomed. But when a long train of abuses and usurpations, pursuing invariably the same Object evinces a design to reduce them under absolute Despotism, it is their right, it is their duty, to throw off such Government, and to provide new Guards for their future security. Such has been the patient sufferance of these Colonies; and such is now the necessity which constrains them to alter their former Systems of Government. The history of the present King of Great Britain is a history of repeated injuries and usurpations, all having in direct object the establishment of an absolute Tyranny over these States. To prove this, let Facts be submitted to a candid world.

He has refused his Assent to Laws, the most wholesome and necessary for the public good.

He has forbidden his Governors to pass Laws of immediate and pressing importance, unless suspended in their operation till his Assent should be obtained; and when so suspended, he has utterly neglected to attend to them.

He has refused to pass other Laws for the accommodation of large districts of people, unless those people would relinquish the right of Representation in the Legislature, a right inestimable to them, and formidable to tyrants only.

He has called together legislative bodies at places unusual, uncomfortable, and distant from the depository of their public Records, for the sole purpose of fatiguing them into compliance with his measures.

He has dissolved Representative Houses repeatedly, for opposing with manly firmness his invasions on the rights of the people.

He has refused for a long time, after such dissolutions, to cause others to be elected; whereby the Legislative powers, incapable of Annihilation, have returned to the People at large for their exercise; the State remaining in the mean time, exposed to all the dangers of invasion from without, and convulsions within.

He has endeavoured to prevent the population of these States; for that purpose obstructing the Laws for Naturalization of Foreigners; refusing to pass others to encourage their migrations hither, and raising the conditions of new Appropriations of Lands.

He has obstructed the Administration of Justice, by refusing his Assent to Laws for establishing Judiciary powers.

He has made Judges dependent on his Will alone, for the tenure of their offices, and the amount and payment of their salaries.

He has erected a multitude of New Offices, and sent hither swarms of Officers, to harass our people, and eat out their substance.

He has kept among us, in times of peace, Standing Armies, without the Consent of our legislatures.

He has affected to render the Military independent of and superior to the Civil power.

He has combined with others to subject us to a jurisdiction foreign to our constitution, and unacknowledged by our laws; giving his Assent to their Acts of pretended Legislation:

For Quartering large bodies of armed troops among us,

For protecting them, by a mock Trial, from punishment for any Murders which they should commit on the Inhabitants of these States,

For cutting off our Trade with all parts of the world,

For imposing Taxes on us without our Consent,

For depriving us, in many cases, of the benefits of Trial by Jury,

For transporting us beyond Seas to be tried for pretended offences,

For abolishing the free System of English Laws in a neighbouring Province, establishing therein an Arbitrary government, and enlarging its Boundaries so as to render it at once an example and fit instrument for introducing the same absolute rule into these Colonies,

For taking away our Charters, abolishing our most valuable Laws, and altering fundamentally the Forms of our

Governments,

For suspending our own Legislatures, and declaring themselves invested with power to legislate for us in all cases whatsoever.

He has abdicated Government here, by declaring us out of his Protection and waging War against us.

He has plundered our seas, ravaged our Coasts, burnt our towns, and destroyed the lives of our people.

He is at this time transporting large Armies of foreign Mercenaries to compleat the works of death, desolation and tyranny, already begun with circumstances of Cruelty & perfidy scarcely paralleled in the most barbarous ages, and totally unworthy the Head of a civilized nation.

He has constrained our fellow Citizens taken Captive on the high Seas to bear Arms against their Country, to become the executioners of their friends and Brethren, or to fall themselves by their Hands.

He has excited domestic insurrections amongst us, and has endeavoured to bring on the inhabitants of our frontiers, the merciless Indian Savages, whose known rule of warfare is an undistinguished destruction of all ages, sexes and conditions.

In every stage of these Oppressions We have Petitioned for Redress in the most humble terms: Our repeated Petitions have been answered only by repeated injury. A Prince whose character is thus marked by every act which may define a Tyrant, is unfit to be the ruler of a free people.

Nor have We been wanting in attentions to our British brethren. We have warned them from time to time of attempts by their legislature to extend an unwarrantable jurisdiction over us. We have reminded them of the circumstances of our emigration and settlement here. We have appealed to their native justice and magnanimity, and we have conjured them by the ties of our common kindred to disavow these usurpations, which, would inevitably interrupt our connections and correspondence. They too have been deaf to the voice of justice and of consanguinity. We must, therefore, acquiesce in the necessity, which denounces our Separation, and hold them, as we hold the rest of mankind, Enemies in War, in Peace Friends.

We, therefore, the Representatives of the united States of America, in General Congress, Assembled, appealing to the Supreme Judge of the world for the rectitude of our intentions, do, in the Name, and by Authority of the good People of these Colonies, solemnly publish and declare, That these United Colonies are, and of Right ought to be, Free and Independent States; that they are Absolved from all Allegiance to the British Crown, and that all political connection between them and the State of Great Britain is and ought to be totally dissolved; and that, as Free and Independent States, they have full Power to levy War, conclude Peace, contract Alliances, establish Commerce, and to do all other Acts and Things which Independent States may of right do. And for the support of this Declaration, with a firm reliance on the protection of divine Providence, we mutually pledge to each other our Lives, our Fortunes and our sacred Honor.

Tecumseh

March 1768 – October 5, 1813

Tecumseh was a Shawnee warrior and chief and is one of the most iconic heroes in Indigenous, American, and Canadian history. Having grown up during the American Revolution and the Northwest Indian War, he sought to form an independent multitribal confederacy east of the Mississippi River that would be under British protection. His confederacy's political and military strength was centered around Prophetstown, the village he founded north of Lafayette, Indiana. The confederation fought the United States in Tecumseh's War, but were defeated and unable to get the government to annul several land cession treaties. Tecumseh's confederation fought the United States again during the War of 1812, in alliance with the British. Tecumseh's death in the Battle of the Thames and the end of the war resulted in the collapse of the pan-Native American alliance.

From Speech to the Osages (1811-1812)

Brothers,—We all belong to one family; we are all children of the Great Spirit; we walk in the same path; slake our thirst at the same spring; and now affairs of the greatest concern lead us to smoke the pipe around the same council fire!

Brothers,—We are friends; we must assist each other to bear our burdens. The blood of many of our fathers and brothers has run like water on the ground, to satisfy the avarice of the white men. We, ourselves, are threatened with a great evil; nothing will pacify them but the destruction of all the red men.

Brothers,—When the white men first set foot on our grounds, they were hungry; they had no place on which to spread their blankets, or to kindle their fires. They were feeble; they could do nothing for themselves. Our fathers commiserated their distress, and shared freely with them whatever the Great Spirit had given his red children. They gave them food when hungry, medicine when sick, spread skins for them to sleep on, and gave them grounds, that they might hunt and raise corn.

Brothers,—The white people are like poisonous serpents: when chilled, they are feeble and harmless; but invigorate them with warmth, and they sting their benefactors to death.

Brothers,—The white people came among us feeble; and now we have made them strong, they wish to kill us, or drive us back, as they would wolves and panthers.

Brothers,—The white men are not friends to the Indians: at first, they only asked for land sufficient for a wigwam; now, nothing will satisfy them but the whole of our hunting grounds, from the rising to the setting sun.

Brothers,—The white men want more than our hunting grounds; they wish to kill our warriors; they would even kill our old men, women and little ones.

Brothers,—Many winters ago, there was no land; the sun did not rise and set: all was darkness. The Great Spirit made all things. He gave the white people a home beyond the great waters. He supplied these grounds with game, and gave them to his red children; and he gave them strength and courage to defend them.

Brothers,—My people wish for peace; the red men all wish for peace; but where the white people are, there is no peace for them, except it be on the bosom of our mother.

Brothers,—The white men despise and cheat the Indians; they abuse and insult them; they do not think the red men sufficiently good to live.

Brothers,—The red men have borne many and great injuries; they ought to suffer them no longer. My people will not; they are determined on vengeance; they have taken up the tomahawk; they will make it fat with blood; they will drink the blood of the white people.

Brothers,—My people are brave and numerous; but the white people are too strong for them alone. I wish you to take up the tomahawk with them. If we all unite, we will cause the rivers to stain the great waters with their blood.

Brothers,—If you do not unite with us, they will first destroy us, and then you will fall an easy prey to them. They have destroyed many nations of red men because they were not united, because they were not friends to each other.

Brothers,—The white people send runners amongst us; they wish to make us enemies that they may sweep over and desolate our hunting grounds, like devastating winds, or rushing waters.

Brothers,—Our Great Father, over the great waters, is angry with the white people, our enemies. He will send his brave warriors against them; he will send us rifles, and whatever else we want—he is our friend, and we are his children.

Brothers,—Who are the white people that we should fear them? They cannot run fast, and are good marks to shoot at: they are only men; our fathers have killed many of them; we are not squaws, and we will stain the earth red with blood.

Brothers,—The Great Spirit is angry with our enemies; he speaks in thunder, and the earth swallows up villages, and drinks up the Mississippi. The great waters will cover their lowlands; their corn cannot grow, and the Great Spirit will sweep those who escape to the hills from the earth with his terrible breach.

Brothers,—We must be united; we must smoke the same pipe; we must fight each other's battles; and more than all, we must love the Great Spirit he is for us; he will destroy our enemies, and make all his red children happy.

Ralph Waldo Emerson

May 25, 1803 – April 27, 1882

Ralph Waldo Emerson was an American poet, essayist, lecturer, and philosopher. He published dozens of essays and gave over fifteen hundred public lectures across America, including his famous Phi Betta Kappa address, "The American Scholar." He was a leader of the transcendentalist movement. A key tenet of transcendentalism is believing in the inherent good of humans and nature. Emerson also stood for individualism, which emphasizes an individual's right to have freedom and the opportunity for self-realization. As a transcendentalist and individualist, Emerson was staunchly opposed to slavery, and gave lectures advocating for abolition. He deeply influenced his contemporaries, who included Walt Whitman, Herman Melville, and Henry David Thoreau. His influence continues today, and he is still considered one of the greatest American philosophers.

From "Self Reliance" (1841)

I read the other day some verses written by an eminent painter which were original and not conventional. The soul always hears an admonition in such lines, let the subject be what it may. The sentiment they instill is of more value than any thought they may contain. To believe your own thought, to believe that what is true for you in your private heart is true for all men,—that is genius. Speak your latent conviction, and it shall be the universal sense; for the inmost in due time becomes the outmost,—and our first thought is rendered back to us by the trumpets of the Last Judgment. Familiar as the voice of the mind is to each, the highest merit we ascribe to Moses, Plato, and Milton is, that they set at naught books and traditions, and spoke not what men but what they thought. A man should learn to detect and watch that gleam of light which flashes across his mind from within, more than the lustre of the firmament of bards and sages. Yet he dismisses without notice his thought, because it is his. In every work of genius we recognize our own rejected thoughts: they come back to us with a certain alienated majesty. Great works of art have no more affecting lesson for us than this. They teach us to abide by our spontaneous impression with good-humored inflexibility than most when the whole cry of voices is on the other side. Else, to-morrow a stranger will say with masterly good sense precisely what we have thought and felt all the time, and we shall be forced to take with shame our own opinion from another.

There is a time in every man's education when he arrives at the conviction that envy is ignorance; that imitation is suicide; that he must take himself for better, for worse, as his portion; that though the wide universe is full of good, no kernel of nourishing corn can come to him but through his toil bestowed on that plot of ground which is given to him to till. The power which resides in him is new in nature, and none but he knows what that is which he can do, nor does he know until he has tried. Not for nothing one face, one character, one fact, makes much impression on him, and another none. This sculpture in the memory is not without preestablished harmony. The eye was placed where one ray should fall, that it might testify of that particular ray. We but half express ourselves, and are ashamed of that divine idea which each of us represents. It may be safely trusted as proportionate and of good issues, so it be faithfully imparted, but God will not have his work made manifest by cowards. A man is relieved and gay when he has put his heart into his work and done his best; but what he has said or done otherwise, shall give him no peace. It is a deliverance which does not deliver. In the attempt his genius deserts him; no muse befriends; no invention, no hope.

Trust thyself: every heart vibrates to that iron string. Accept the place the divine providence has found for you, the society of your contemporaries, the connection of events. Great men have always done so, and confided themselves childlike to the genius of their age, betraying their perception that the absolutely trustworthy was seated at their heart, working through their hands, predominating in all their being. And we are now men, and must accept in the highest mind the same transcendent destiny; and not minors and invalids in a protected corner, not cowards fleeing before a revolution, but guides, redeemers, and benefactors, obeying the Almighty effort, and advancing on Chaos and the Dark.

Elizabeth Cady Stanton

November 12, 1815 – October 26, 1902

Elizabeth Cady Stanton was an abolitionist, women's rights activist, and—alongside Susan B. Anthony—a leader in the women's suffrage movement. She was a primary author of the Declaration of Sentiments, which is credited with motivating the first organized women's rights and suffrage movements in the United States. Stanton worked to secure women's right to divorce, access to birth control, parental and custody rights, property rights, and employment and income rights. After the Civil War, her and Anthony's opposition to the Fifteenth Amendment, which gave the right to vote to freed Black men but not to any women, caused a rift in these movements. Stanton later became the president of the National American Woman Suffrage Association.

From The Seneca Falls Declaration of Sentiments (1848)

When, in the course of human events, it becomes necessary for one portion of the family of man to assume among the people of the earth a position different from that which they have hitherto occupied, but one to which the laws of nature and of nature's God entitle them, a decent respect to the opinions of mankind requires that they should declare the causes that impel them to such a course.

We hold these truths to be self-evident: that all men and women are created equal; that they are endowed by their Creator with certain inalienable rights; that among these are life, liberty, and the pursuit of happiness; that to secure these rights governments are instituted, deriving their just powers from the consent of the governed. Whenever any form of Government becomes destructive of these ends, it is the right of those who suffer from it to refuse allegiance to it, and to insist upon the institution of a new government, laying its foundation on such principles, and organizing its powers in such form as to them shall seem most likely to effect their safety and happiness. Prudence, indeed, will dictate that governments long established should not be changed for light and transient causes; and accordingly, all experience hath shown that mankind are more disposed to suffer, while evils are sufferable, than to right themselves by abolishing the forms to which they are accustomed. But when a long train of abuses and usurpations, pursuing invariably the same object, evinces a design to reduce them under absolute despotism, it is their duty to throw off such government, and to provide new guards for their future security. Such has been the patient sufferance of the women under this government, and such is now the necessity which constrains them to demand the equal station to which they are entitled.

The history of mankind is a history of repeated injuries and usurpations on the part of man toward woman, having in direct object the establishment of an absolute tyranny over her. To prove this, let facts be submitted to a candid world.

He has never permitted her to exercise her inalienable right to the elective franchise.

He has compelled her to submit to laws, in the formation of which she had no voice.

He has withheld from her rights which are given to the most ignorant and degraded men—both natives and foreigners.

Having deprived her of this first right of a citizen, the elective franchise, thereby leaving her without representation in the halls of legislation, he has oppressed her on all sides.

He has made her, if married, in the eye of the law, civilly dead.

He has taken from her all right in property, even to the

wages she earns.

He has made her, morally, an irresponsible being, as she can commit many crimes with impunity, provided they be done in the presence of her husband. In the covenant of marriage, she is compelled to promise obedience to her husband, he becoming, to all intents and purposes, her master—the law giving him power to deprive her of her liberty, and to administer chastisement.

He has so framed the laws of divorce, as to what shall be the proper causes of divorce; in case of separation, to whom the guardianship of the children shall be given; as to be wholly regardless of the happiness of women—the law, in all cases, going upon the false supposition of the supremacy of man, and giving all power into his hands.

After depriving her of all rights as a married woman, if single and the owner of property, he has taxed her to support a government which recognizes her only when her property can be made profitable to it.

He has monopolized nearly all the profitable employments, and from those she is permitted to follow, she receives but a scanty remuneration.

He closes against her all the avenues to wealth and distinction, which he considers most honorable to himself. As a teacher of theology, medicine, or law, she is not known.

He has denied her the facilities for obtaining a thorough education—all colleges being closed against her.

He allows her in Church as well as State, but a subordinate position, claiming Apostolic authority for her exclusion from the ministry, and, with some exceptions, from any public participation in the affairs of the Church.

He has created a false public sentiment, by giving to the world a different code of morals for men and women, by which moral delinquencies which exclude women from society, are not only tolerated but deemed of little account in man.

He has usurped the prerogative of Jehovah himself, claiming it as his right to assign for her a sphere of action, when that belongs to her conscience and her God.

He has endeavored, in every way that he could to destroy her confidence in her own powers, to lessen her self-respect, and to make her willing to lead a dependent and abject life.

Now, in view of this entire disfranchisement of one-half the people of this country, their social and religious degradation,—in view of the unjust laws above mentioned, and because women do feel themselves aggrieved, oppressed, and fraudulently deprived of their most sacred rights, we insist that they have immediate admission to all the rights and privileges which belong to them as citizens of these United States.

In entering upon the great work before us, we anticipate no small amount of misconception, misrepresentation, and ridicule; but we shall use every instrumentality within our power to effect our object. We shall employ agents, circulate tracts, petition the State and national Legislatures, and endeavor to enlist the pulpit and the press in our behalf. We hope this Convention will be followed by a series of Conventions, embracing every part of the country.

Firmly relying upon the final triumph of the Right and the True, we do this day affix our signatures to this declaration.

Henry David Thoreau

July 12, 1817 – May 6, 1862

Henry David Thoreau was an American philosopher, essayist, and poet. He is best known for his book *Walden* and his essay "Civil Disobedience." Thoreau was a leading transcendentalist and he wrote over twenty volumes of journals, essays, and poetry expounding on ecology, philosophy, and political change. Thoreau was a lifelong abolitionist and was a conductor on the Underground Railroad. He fervently attacked the Fugitive Slave Law, and defended fellow abolitionist John Brown, who led a raid on the federal armory at Harper's Ferry, Virginia. Considered by some to be an anarchist, Thoreau actually called for the improvement of government rather than its abolition. Thoreau's philosophy and politics influenced his contemporaries and went on to inspire the likes of Leo Tolstoy, Mahatma Gandhi, and Martin Luther King, Jr.

From "Civil Disobedience" (1849)

After all, the practical reason why, when the power is once in the hands of the people, a majority are permitted, and for a long period continue, to rule is not because they are most likely to be in the right, nor because this seems fairest to the minority, but because they are physically the strongest. But a government in which the majority rule in all cases cannot be based on justice, even as far as men understand it. Can there not be a government in which majorities do not virtually decide right and wrong, but conscience?—in which majorities decide only those questions to which the rule of expediency is applicable? Must the citizen ever for a moment, or in the least degree, resign his conscience to the legislation? Why has every man a conscience, then? I think that we should be men first, and subjects afterward. It is not desirable to cultivate a respect for the law, so much as for the right. The only obligation which I have a right to assume is to do at any time what I think right. . . .

It is not a man's duty, as a matter of course, to devote himself to the eradication of any, even the most enormous, wrong; he may still properly have other concerns to engage him; but it is his duty, at least, to wash his hands of it, and, if he gives it no thought longer, not to give it practically his support. If I devote myself to other pursuits and contemplations, I must first see, at least, that I do not pursue them sitting upon another man's shoulders. I must get off him first, that he may pursue his contemplations too. See what gross inconsistency is tolerated. I have heard some of my townsmen say, "I should like to have them order me out to help put down an insurrection of the slaves, or to march to Mexico;—see if I would go"; and yet these very men have each, directly by their allegiance, and so indirectly, at least, by their money, furnished a substitute. The soldier is applauded who refuses to serve in an unjust war by those who do not refuse to sustain the unjust government which makes the war; is applauded by those whose own act and authority he disregards and sets at naught; as if the state were penitent to that degree that it differed one to scourge it while it sinned, but not to that degree that it left off sinning for a moment. Thus, under the name of Order and Civil Government, we are all made at last to pay homage to and support our own meanness. After the first blush of sin comes its indifference; and from immoral it becomes, as it were, unmoral, and not quite unnecessary to that life which we have made. . . .

Unjust laws exist: shall we be content to obey them, or shall we endeavor to amend them, and obey them until we have succeeded, or shall we transgress them at once? Men generally, under such a government as this, think that they ought to wait until they have persuaded the majority to alter them. They think that, if they should resist, the remedy would be worse than the evil. But it is the fault of the government itself that the remedy is worse than the evil. It makes it worse. Why is it not more apt to anticipate and provide for reform? Why does it not cherish its wise minority? Why does it cry and resist before it is hurt? Why does it not encourage its citizens to be on the alert to point out its faults, and do better than it would have them? Why does it always crucify Christ, and excommunicate Copernicus and Luther, and pronounce Washington and Franklin rebels? . . .

If the injustice is part of the necessary friction of the machine of government, let it go, let it go: perchance it will wear smooth—certainly the machine will wear out. If the injustice has a spring, or a pulley, or a rope, or a crank, exclusively for itself, then perhaps you may consider whether the remedy will not be worse than the evil; but if it is of such a nature that it requires you to be the agent of injustice to another, then, I say, break the law. Let your life be a counter-friction to stop the machine. What I have to do is to see, at any rate, that I do not lend myself to the wrong which I condemn.

Sojourner Truth

c. 1797 – November 26, 1883

Sojourner Truth was a Black abolitionist and women's rights advocate, known for highlighting racial inequalities in America in her speech "Ain't I a Woman?" Truth escaped from slavery in 1826 with her infant daughter and took her former owner to court in 1828 to recover her son, becoming one of the first Black women to win such a case against a white man. Although advocating for freedom and equality was dangerous, especially for a once-enslaved woman, Truth devoted her life to the cause of abolition and helped recruit black troops for the Union Army during the Civil War. She also supported prison reform, property rights, and universal suffrage. In 2014, she was included in Smithsonian magazine's "100 Most Significant Americans of All Time" list.

From "Ain't I a Woman?" (1851)

Well, children, where there is so much racket there must be something out of kilter. I think that `twixt the negroes of the South and the women at the North, all talking about rights, the white men will be in a fix pretty soon. But what's all this here talking about?

That man over there says that women need to be helped into carriages, and lifted over ditches, and to have the best place everywhere. Nobody ever helps me into carriages, or over mud-puddles, or gives me any best place! And ain't I a woman? Look at me! Look at my arm! I have ploughed and planted, and gathered into barns, and no man could head me! And ain't I a woman? I could work as much and eat as much as a man—when I could get it—and bear the lash as well! And ain't I a woman? I have borne thirteen children, and seen most all sold off to slavery, and when I cried out with my mother's grief, none but Jesus heard me! And ain't I a woman?

Then they talk about this thing in the head; what's this they call it? [Member of audience whispers, "intellect."] That's it, honey. What's that got to do with women's rights or negroes' rights? If my cup won't hold but a pint, and yours holds a quart, wouldn't you be mean not to let me have my little half measure full?

Then that little man in black there, he says women can't have as much rights as men, 'cause Christ wasn't a woman! Where did your Christ come from? Where did your Christ come from? From God and a woman! Man had nothing to do with Him.

If the first woman God ever made was strong enough to turn the world upside down all alone, these women together ought to be able to turn it back, and get it right side up again! And now they is asking to do it, the men better let them.

Obliged to you for hearing me, and now old Sojourner ain't got nothing more to say.

Frederick Douglass

February 1818 – February 20, 1895

Frederick Douglass escaped as a young man from slavery in Maryland and became one of the most renowned orators, writers, and social reformers in American history. He was an essential leader of the abolitionist movement and, believing in the equality of all people, also advocated for the rights of Native Americans, women, and immigrants. His success and skill as a speaker, writer, and leader was evidence against the commonly held belief that slaves lacked the intellectual capacity to be independent and free. Douglass believed in the power of words to create change and used dialogue to break down racial and ideological barriers. He explained his beliefs and strategies in one simple sentence: "I would unite with anybody to do right and with nobody to do wrong."

From "What, to the Slave, is the Fourth of July" (1852)

. . . The papers and placards say, that I am to deliver a 4th [of] July oration. This certainly sounds large and out of the common way, for me. It is true that I have often had the privilege to speak in this beautiful Hall, and to address many who now honor me with their presence. But neither their familiar faces, nor the perfect gage I think I have of Corinthian Hall, seems to free me from embarrassment.

The fact is, ladies and gentlemen, the distance between this platform and the slave plantation, from which I escaped, is considerable—and the difficulties to be overcome in getting from the latter to the former, are by no means slight. That I am here today, is, to me, a matter of astonishment as well as of gratitude. . . .

. . .Oppression makes a wise man mad. Your fathers

Frederick Douglass (1818-1895), a former slave, was widely known for his anti-slavery oratory, writing, and leadership of the abolitionist movement.
LIBRARY OF CONGRESS, LCUSZ62-15887

were wise men, and if they did not go mad, they became restive under this treatment. They felt themselves the victims of grievous wrongs, wholly incurable in their colonial capacity. With brave men there is always a remedy for oppression. Just here, the idea of a total separation of the colonies from the crown was born! It was a startling idea, much more so, than we, at this distance of time, regard it. The timid and the prudent (as has been intimated) of that day, were, of course, shocked and alarmed by it. . . .

. . . Fellow Citizens, I am not wanting in respect for the fathers of this republic. The signers of the Declaration of Independence were brave men. They were great men too-great enough to give fame to a great age. It does not often happen to a nation to raise, at one time, such a number of truly great men. The point from which I am compelled to view them is not, certainly the most favorable; and yet I cannot contemplate their great deeds with less than admiration. They were statesmen, patriots and heroes, and for the good they did, and the principles they contended for, I will unite with you to honor their memory. . . .

We have to do with the past only as we can make it useful to the present and to the future. To all inspiring motives, to noble deeds which can be gained from the past, we are welcome. But now is the time, the important time. Your fathers have lived, died, and have done their work, and have done much of it well. You live and must die, and you must do your work. You have no right to enjoy a child's share in the labor of your fathers, unless your children are to be blest by your labors. You have no right to wear out and waste the hard-earned fame of your fathers to cover your indolence. Sydney Smith tells us that men seldom eulogize the wisdom and virtues of their fathers, but to excuse some folly or wickedness of their own. This truth is not a doubtful one. There are illustrations of it near and remote, ancient and modern. It was fashionable, hundreds of years ago, for the children of Jacob to boast, we have "Abraham to our father," when they had long lost Abraham's faith and spirit. That people contented themselves under the shadow of Abraham's great name, while they repudiated the deeds which made his name great. Need I remind you that a similar thing is being done all over this country today? Need I tell you that the Jews are not the only people who built the tombs of the prophets, and garnished the sepulchres of the righteous? Washington could not die till he had broken the chains of his slaves. Yet his monument is built up by the price of human blood, and the traders in the bodies and souls of men, shout— "We have Washington to *our father.*" Alas! that it should be so; yet so it is.

> *The evil that men do, lives after them, The good is oft interred with their bones.*

Fellow-citizens, pardon me, allow me to ask, why am I called upon to speak here today? What have I, or those I represent, to do with your national independence? Are the great principles of political freedom and of natural justice, embodied in that Declaration of Independence, extended to us? and am I, therefore, called upon to bring our humble offering to the national altar, and to confess the benefits and express devout gratitude for the blessings resulting from your independence to us?

Would to God, both for your sakes and ours, that an

affirmative answer could be truthfully returned to these questions! Then would my task be light, and my burden easy and delightful. For who is there so cold, that a nation's sympathy could not warm him? Who so obdurate and dead to the claims of gratitude, that would not thankfully acknowledge such priceless benefits? Who so stolid and selfish, that would not give his voice to swell the hallelujahs of a nation's jubilee, when the chains of servitude had been torn from his limbs? I am not that man. In a case like that, the dumb might eloquently speak, and the "lame man leap as an hart."

But, such is not the state of the case. I say it with a sad sense of the disparity between us. I am not included within the pale of this glorious anniversary! Your high independence only reveals the immeasurable distance between us. The blessings in which you, this day, rejoice, are not enjoyed in common.—The rich inheritance of justice, liberty, prosperity and independence, bequeathed by your fathers, is shared by you, not by me. The sunlight that brought life and healing to you, has brought stripes and death to me. This Fourth [of] July is yours, not mine. You may rejoice, I must mourn. To drag a man in fetters into the grand illuminated temple of liberty, and call upon him to join you in joyous anthems, were inhuman mockery and sacrilegious irony. Do you mean, citizens, to mock me, by asking me to speak today? If so, there is a parallel to your conduct. And let me warn you that it is dangerous to copy the example of a nation whose crimes, towering up to heaven, were thrown down by the breath of the Almighty, burying that nation in irrecoverable ruin! I can today take up the plaintive lament of a peeled and woe-smitten people!

"By the rivers of Babylon, there we sat down. Yea! we wept when we remembered Zion. We hanged our harps upon the willows in the midst thereof. For there, they that carried us away captive, required of us a song; and they who wasted us required of us mirth, saying, Sing us one of the songs of Zion. How can we sing the Lord's song in a strange land? If I forget thee, O Jerusalem, let my right hand forget her cunning. If I do not remember thee, let my tongue cleave to the roof of my mouth."

Fellow-citizens; above your national, tumultuous joy, I hear the mournful wail of millions! whose chains, heavy and grievous yesterday, are, today, rendered more intolerable by the jubilee shouts that reach them. If I do forget, if I do not faithfully remember those bleeding children of sorrow this day, "may my right hand forget her cunning, and may my tongue cleave to the roof of my mouth!" To forget them, to pass lightly over their wrongs, and to chime in with the popular theme, would be treason most scandalous and shocking, and would make me a reproach before God and the world. My subject, then, fellow-citizens, is AMERICAN SLAVERY. I shall see, this day, and its popular characteristics, from the slave's point of view. Standing, there, identified with the American bondman, making his wrongs mine, I do not hesitate to declare, with all my soul, that the character and conduct of this nation never looked blacker to me than on this 4th of July! Whether we turn to the declarations of the past, or to the professions of the present, the conduct of the nation seems equally hideous and revolting. America is false to the past, false to the present, and solemnly binds herself to be false to the future. Standing with God and the crushed and bleeding slave on this occasion, I will, in the name of humanity which is outraged, in the name of liberty which is fettered, in the name of the constitution and the Bible, which are disregarded and trampled upon, dare to call in question and to denounce, with all the emphasis I can command, everything that serves to perpetuate slavery—the great sin and shame of America! "I will not equivocate; I will not excuse"; I will use the severest language I can command; and yet not one word shall escape me that any man, whose judgment is not blinded by prejudice, or who is not at heart a slaveholder, shall not confess to be right and just.

But I fancy I hear some one of my audience say, it is just in this circumstance that you and your brother abolitionists fail to make a favorable impression on the public mind. Would you argue more, and denounce less, would you persuade more, and rebuke less, your cause would be much more likely to succeed. But, I submit, where all is plain there is nothing to be argued. What point in the anti-slavery creed would you have me argue? On what branch of the subject do the people of this country need light? Must I undertake to prove that the slave is a man? That point is conceded already. Nobody doubts it. The slave-holders themselves acknowledge it in the enactment of laws for their government. They acknowledge it when they punish disobedience on the part of the slave. There are seventy two crimes in the State of Virginia, which, if committed by a black man, (no matter how ignorant he be), subject him to the punishment of death; while only two of the same crimes will subject a white man to the like punishment.—What is this but the acknowledgement that the slave is a moral, intellectual and responsible being. The manhood of the slave is conceded. It is admitted in the fact that Southern statute books are covered with enactments forbidding, under severe fines and penalties, the teaching of the slave to read or to write.—When you can point to any such laws, in reference to the beasts of the field, then I may consent to argue the manhood of the slave. When the dogs in your streets, when the fowls of the air, when the cattle on your hills, when the fish of the sea, and the reptiles that crawl, shall be unable to distinguish the slave from a brute, then will I argue with you that the slave is a man!

For the present, it is enough to affirm the equal manhood of the negro race. Is it not astonishing that, while we are ploughing, planting and reaping, using all kinds of mechanical tools, erecting houses, constructing bridges, building ships, working in metals of brass, iron, copper, silver and gold; that, while we are reading, writing and cyphering, acting as clerks, merchants and secretaries, having among us lawyers, doctors, ministers, poets, authors, editors, orators and teachers; that, while we are engaged in all manner of enterprises common to other men, digging gold in California, capturing the whale in the Pacific, feeding sheep and cattle on the hillside, living, moving, acting, thinking, planning, living in families as husbands, wives and children, and, above all, confessing and worshipping the Christian's God, and looking hopefully for life and immortality beyond the grave, we are called upon to prove that we are men!

Would you have me argue that man is entitled to liberty? that he is the rightful owner of his own body? You have already declared it. Must I argue the wrongfulness of slavery? Is that a question for Republicans? Is it to be settled by the rules of logic and argumentation, as a matter beset with great difficulty, involving a doubtful application of the principle of justice, hard to be understood? How should I look today, in the presence of Americans, dividing, and subdividing a discourse, to show that men have a natural right to freedom? speaking of it relatively, and positively, negatively, and affirmatively. To do so, would be to make myself ridiculous, and to offer an insult to your understanding.—There is not a man beneath the canopy of heaven, that does not know that slavery is wrong *for him*.

What, am I to argue that it is wrong to make men brutes, to rob them of their liberty, to work them without wages, to keep them ignorant of their relations to their fellow men, to beat them with sticks, to flay their flesh with the lash, to load their limbs with irons, to hunt them with dogs, to sell them at auction, to sunder their families, to knock out their teeth, to burn their flesh, to starve them into obedience and submission to their masters? Must I argue that a system thus marked with blood, and stained with pollution, is wrong? No I will not. I have better employment for my time and strength, than such arguments would imply.

What, then, remains to be argued? Is it that slavery is not divine; that God did not establish it; that our doctors of divinity are mistaken? There is blasphemy in the thought. That which is inhuman, cannot be divine! Who can reason on such a proposition? They that can, may; I cannot. The time for such argument is past.

At a time like this, scorching irony, not convincing argument, is needed. O! had I the ability, and could I reach the nation's ear, I would, to day, pour out a fiery stream of biting ridicule, blasting reproach, withering sarcasm, and stern rebuke. For it is not light that is needed, but fire; it is not the gentle shower, but thunder. We need the storm, the whirlwind, and the earthquake. The feeling of the nation must be quickened; the conscience of the nation must be roused; the propriety of the nation must be startled; the hypocrisy of the nation must be exposed; and its crimes against God and man must be proclaimed and denounced.

What, to the American slave, is your 4th of July? I answer; a day that reveals to him, more than all other days in the year, the gross injustice and cruelty to which he is the constant victim. To him, your celebration is a sham; your boasted liberty, an unholy license; your national greatness, swelling vanity; your sounds of rejoicing are empty and heartless; your denunciations of tyrants, brass fronted impudence; your shouts of liberty and equality, hollow mockery; your prayers and hymns, your sermons and thanksgivings, with all your religious parade, and solemnity, are, to him, mere bombast, fraud, deception, impiety, and hypocrisy—a thin veil to cover up crimes which would disgrace a nation of savages. There is not a nation on the earth guilty of practices, more shocking and bloody, than are the people of these United States, at this very hour.

. . . Allow me to say, in conclusion, notwithstanding the dark picture I have this day presented, of the state of the nation, I do not despair of this country. There are forces in operation, which must inevitably, work the downfall of slavery. "The arm of the Lord is not shortened," and the doom of slavery is certain. I, therefore, leave off where I began, with hope. While drawing encouragement from "the Declaration of Independence," the great principles it contains, and the genius of American Institutions, my spirit is also cheered by the obvious tendencies of the age. Nations do not now stand in the same relation to each other that they did ages ago. No nation can now shut itself up, from the surrounding world, and trot round in the same old path of its fathers without interference. The time was when such could be done. Long established customs of hurtful character could formerly fence themselves in, and do their evil work with social impunity. Knowledge was then confined and enjoyed by the privileged few, and the multitude walked on in mental darkness. But a change has now come over the affairs of mankind. Walled cities and empires have become unfashionable. The arm of commerce has borne away the gates of the strong city. Intelligence is penetrating the darkest corners of the globe. It makes its pathway over and under the sea, as well as on the earth. Wind, steam, and lightning are its chartered agents. Oceans no longer divide, but link nations together. From Boston to London is now a holiday excursion. Space is comparatively annihilated.— Thoughts expressed on one side of the Atlantic, are distinctly heard on the other. . . .

Abraham Lincoln

February 12, 1809 – April 15, 1865

Abraham Lincoln was a lawyer and statesman before being elected the sixteenth president of the United States. His presidency was defined by the American Civil War. The Civil War was America's bloodiest war to date and posed greatest moral and constitutional crisis. Lincoln was able to preserve the Union, abolish slavery, and modernize the country's economy. He avoided retribution against the secessionists, hoping the two sides of the damaged nation could reconcile. Lincoln was assassinated by John Wilkes Booth in April 1865. He is remembered as a hero and counted among the greatest American presidents by the public and scholars alike.

From Second Inaugural Address (1865)

Fellow Countrymen,

At this second appearing to take the oath of the presidential office, there is less occasion for an extended address than there was at the first. Then a statement, somewhat in detail, of a course to be pursued, seemed fitting and proper. Now, at the expiration of four years, during which public declarations have been constantly called forth on every point and phase of the great contest which still absorbs the attention, and engrosses the enerergies of the nation, little that is new could be presented. The progress of our arms, upon which all else chiefly depends, is as well known to the public as to myself; and it is, I trust, reasonably satisfactory and encouraging to all. With high hope for the future, no prediction in regard to it is ventured.

On the occasion corresponding to this four years ago, all thoughts were anxiously directed to an impending civil-war.

All dreaded it—all sought to avert it. While the inaugural address was being delivered from this place, devoted altogether to saving the Union without war, insurgent agents were in the city seeking to destroy it without war—seeking to dissolve the Union, and divide effects, by negotiation. Both parties deprecated war; but one of them would make war rather than let the nation survive; and the other would accept war rather than let it perish. And the war came.

One-eighth of the whole population were colored slaves, not distributed generally over the Union, but localized in the Southern half part of it. These slaves constituted a peculiar and powerful interest. All knew that this interest was, somehow, the cause of the war. To strengthen, perpetuate, and extend this interest was the object for which the insurgents would rend the Union, even by war; while the government claimed no right to do more than to restrict the territorial enlargement of it. Neither party expected for the war, the magnitude, or the duration, which it has already attained. Neither anticipated that the cause of the conflict might cease with, or even before, the conflict itself should cease. Each looked for an easier triumph, and a result less fundamental and astounding. Both read the same Bible, and pray to the same God; and each invokes His aid against the other. It may seem strange that any men should dare to ask a just God's assistance in wringing their bread from the sweat of other men's faces; but let us judge not that we be not judged. The prayers of both could not be answered; that of neither has been answered fully. The Almighty has His own purposes. "Woe unto the world because of offences! for it must needs be that offences come; but woe to that man by whom the offence cometh!" If we shall suppose that American Slavery is one of those offences which, in the providence of God, must needs come, but which, having continued through His appointed time, He now wills to remove, and that He gives to both North and South, this terrible war, as the woe due to those by whom the offence came, shall we discern therein any departure from those divine attributes which the believers in a Living God always ascribe to Him? Fondly do we hope—fervently do we pray—that this mighty scourge of war may speedily pass away. Yet, if God wills that it continue, until all the wealth piled by the bondman's two hundred and fifty years of unrequited toil shall be sunk, and until every drop of blood drawn with the lash, shall be paid by another drawn with the sword, as was said three thousand years ago, so still it must be said "the judgments of the Lord, are true and righteous altogether."

With malice toward none; with charity for all; with firmness in the right, as God gives us to see the right, let us strive on to finish the work we are in; to bind up the nation's wounds; to care for him who shall have borne the battle, and for his widow, and his orphan—to do all which may achieve and cherish a just, and a lasting peace, among ourselves, and with all nations.

Wyoming Context

Peter Kooi Simpson

Historian and politician, Pete Simpson, is a beloved member of the Simpson political family. A native of Cody, Simpson's immediate family includes a governor and a senator.

In 1953, Pete Simpson graduated from the University of Wyoming with the first of three history degrees. After four years in the Navy, Pete starred in a local television program in Billings, Montana. He worked in administration at Casper College and then Dean of Instruction at Sheridan College. He was twice elected to the Wyoming House of Representatives from 1981-84. In 1986, Simpson was the Wyoming Republican gubernatorial nominee.

In Laramie, he served as UW Vice President for Institutional Advancement and Executive Director of the University of Wyoming Foundation then as Simpson Distinguished Professor of Political Sciences, teaching until 2012. Pete continues to participate in cultural and civic affairs and hosts the "Pete Simpson Forum" in the online newspaper, *WyoFile*.

From Address to the Wyoming Humanities Council (2013)

I was at one time one of you—a human. No, a member of the Wyoming Humanities Council, though I'm reminded of Groucho Marx's comment that his mother loved children and "She would have given anything had I been one."

Well, I'm sure I'm like all alumni of the council when I say it's very much like getting back with close friends who share similar values and similar perspectives and are devoted to the common cause of purveying those values and perspectives to our fellow citizens.

These are big challenges. But as Timothy Geithner said when he was first put on the firing line as Secretary of the

Treasury before Congress, "If a challenge, it wouldn't be consequential." (I'll bet he wished he'd never said that.) There are consequences in the challenges before the council at this important juncture, and the session tomorrow can make them truly consequential and profoundly beneficial for the council and for the state of Wyoming.

So what are these humanities to us in Wyoming? No way to answer that unless we know what they are for all of humankind. You have, I believe, a wonderful interview with the president of the Mellon Foundation—a remarkable man, Don Randel, former president of the University of Chicago and renowned musicologist. His essay on the value and worth of the humanities is rousing and eloquent.

I'd like to emphasize a couple of his points here tonight: first, his contention that the exercise of our minds and our creative spirit is a basic human right, and second, in that exercise we should acknowledge the primacy of ideas and take them seriously. "Ideas change the world." To take them seriously is to be thoughtful, and there is nothing we need more at this juncture of human history than to be more thoughtful societies—societies in which ideas matter and inform our public discourse, broadening our understanding of issues, helping us to become more creative problem solvers and wiser decision-makers.

I'm always reminded of that old epigram of the young neophyte and the old sage where the young man asks, "Old man, old man, how are you so wise?"

And the old man replies, "Good judgment, young man, good judgement!"

And the young man rejoins, "Old man, old man, how do you get good judgement?"

"Experience, young man, experience."

"Old man, old man, how do you get experience?'

"Poor judgement, young man, poor judgment!"

Democracy Under Construction

Well, allegorically, the story points to the need to learn from the earliest age. For Randel, the humanities ought to be taught in pre-school and ought to be a part of the lives of everyone from the cradle to the grave.

For the ancient Greeks, you were not a human at conception or at birth. You were fully human only when you were a part of the polis—the public body of your fellow humans—and, you had to participate in the polis to gain that humanness. They assumed that reason would be the basis for that participation. But, Randel acknowledges that, and I quote him, "there is a deeply anti-intellectual streak in the life of the nation." That's a condition that the humanities can and must combat. In order to preserve the democracy, the polity demands a rational, creative approach. Indeed, in America's case, it was founded on it. And, we must fuel the side that stands for that equation. The humanities are our intellectual broadswords to fight ignorance, cynicism, trivialization, and complacency, and the more and better ways we contrive to wield them, the more we meet our responsibility to our citizens.

My brother Al Simpson's definition of politics applies here—not the one where he says politics is the marriage of two words, the Latin *poly* which means "many," and the word *tic* which is a blood-sucking insect. No, the more thoughtful one that describes the political process as follows:

> In politics, there are no right answers, just a continuing flow of compromises resulting in a changing, cloudy, and ambiguous series of public decisions where appetite and ambition compete openly with knowledge and wisdom.

The humanities can and do expose appetite and ambition, as Thucydides did in his *History of the Peloponnesian Wars* by reciting the argument in the Athenian senate against attacking the neutral island of Melos. Athens paid dearly for doing that. And, the humanities can and do nourish knowledge and wisdom as they did when the noted French humanist and writer Émil Zola came to the defense of the wrongfully convicted Captain Alfred Dreyfus in the late nineteenth century—an event widely marked as a prominent example of the power of intellectuals to shape public opinion.

The Wyoming Humanities Council has not been a stranger to these sorts of causes. To the contrary, you've initiated some admirable projects to awaken understanding and promote tolerance. I allude to the forum discussing Islamic history for Wyomingites after 9-11 and the lecture addressing the topic of "wolves and men" a few years ago (something else that could be done again), and for confronting the ramifications of America's gun culture in the program *God, Google, and Guns* as a component of "Civility Matters" [a previous Wyoming Humanities program]. But,—now I may make some of us uncomfortable—has there been any exploration of the relationship between accessibility and the high ownership of guns to Wyoming's high suicide rate, the highest in the nation?

Political cartoons are another form of expression in civil dialogues. In 1869, Wyoming led the way with the first established women's suffrage law enacted in the United States.

WYOMING STATE ARCHIVES, DEPARTMENT OF STATE PARKS AND CULTURAL RESOURCES

I bring this up because I've heard that suicide is one of Governor Matt Mead's top social concerns. And since one of the keys to the funding that the state has provided to the council is civic engagement, the council might appropriately tackle that issue either through a forum or a conference since, as we all know, for any Wyoming politician to tackle any issue that even might smell like an infringement on Second Amendment rights is to commit political suicide We can certainly see why the governor is looking toward the council. And, if done right, a discussion could inform decision makers and help the state to know better how to deal with this serious health problem, which it clearly is.

And while I'm listing commendations for the Wyoming Humanities Council projects that deal with critical public issues, I'd like to mention the Civility Year that attended National Endowment for the Humanities Chairman Leach's three-year civility tour ending in 2011. These projects were illuminating and well received, but I can't help think of continuing to pursue the concept in real time, putting the concept of civility to the test in more open forums on hot-button issues in the years ahead (the demise of the post office, consolidation of public schools, etc.) and recruiting facilitators who can claim some experience and expertise at that very demanding skill—holding down the temperature while encouraging dialogue.

Is that possible here in Wyoming at a time of national divisions that have cut deeper into our sense of oneness than at any time in my memory—and I'm developing a long run on my memory (it's just the short term that gives me trouble).

Is that possible in the public forum in Wyoming, at a time of single-party control? The Wyoming legislature numbers twelve Democrats out of ninety lawmakers in Cheyenne—87% are Republican. In Cody last April, the city planning meeting was broken up by Tea Party agitators. In other words, is it worth it to disagree with the majority? Or, with anyone? Even, sometimes, is it safe?

I have contended in an article regarding civility here in

Wyoming that civility matters in this state, because it has to. We're too few in number and we know each other too well, and we are more intimately connected than in larger, more urban states. We have to get along, as John Perry Barlow once wrote in an essay on Wyoming. We have to be careful after an argument because, sure as the devil, you might be stuck out on Shirley Rim in a blinding blizzard and the first guy to come along is the guy you've had the brush with and you have to, as the old cowboy says, "heal up and hair over."

I can't help but think that more statewide public forums bringing the humanities to bear on state wide issues and conducted by experienced facilitators will lead to more civic engagement. And, I can't imagine a time when we need a more engaged citizenry than now.

I have some encouraging precedents to cite for such a format. I had the privilege and pleasure to teach two political science courses at the University of Wyoming. One was called Wyoming's Political Identity, and it was largely conducted as an open forum wherein students were given a weekly topic list of issues with a humanities focus—historical backgrounding primarily. And, the students were asked to write response papers for the next meeting of the class, from which discussion of those issues took place. They had to research the issues and think about them because their fellow students would be addressing them too and their participation counted points.

Over the years, there were town kids in the class and ranch kids; foreign students; students from California, New York, Vermont, Colorado, you name it; older students; single mothers; Native Americans; and representatives of every race and creed—a less homogeneous population than Wyoming at large and, in some ways, an even bigger challenge to make the class experience both civil and safe.

I learned a lot in the twelve years I taught that class: a lot about listening, about acknowledging opinions without necessarily endorsing them, about recognizing each student's individuality—remembering their names, for example (is that common sense? Of course it is!),—and most importantly about finding common ground wherever possible.

And, one thing more! It helps mightily if the venue is auditorium-style—preferably a semi-circle of seating. People have to look at each other when they talk—sort of "engineered" civility, civility by design.

There were brisk discussions, stimulating arguments, energetic exchanges—and all without thrown chairs or fisticuffs. Indeed, there were even some topics forwarded to the state legislature. The tobacco tax actually came from research done by students in the second class I taught, a public policy class called Wyoming Futures. And the House took the research and ran with it. We had a mini-public policy institute going there for a while. It was a revelation and encouraged me about the next generation. In fact, three of those students became state legislators in Cheyenne, and two of them,— minority leader Patrick Goggles and House Education Committee Chair, Matt Teeters—are still there.

The Wyoming Humanities Council are the conveners. You can and do convene groups and agencies and leaders and thinkers. You are second to none in organizing forums and conferences. Might not statewide public policy issues forums be taken on the road with a reasonable number of visits to various towns with a schedule and advance literature—like Buffalo Bill's show *Je Viens*, (I am coming)—and the towns selected know what's going to be discussed?

These events could be like a conference on public affairs, tapping public policy leaders, selected humanists, political analysts (a nationally recognized spokesperson or expert)— something along the lines of the Social Science Seminars at Casper College in the 1970s—or open discussions with top scholars and political figures. But they should be into thoughtful policy formulation. We're not a chamber of commerce.

What sorts of larger issues might be addressed? If I were ever asked about a major issue affecting all of us in Wyoming and nationwide (and I think the council's effort to survey constituents about important issues is a first-rate exercise), I would choose rising economic inequality. As a nation, we have accomplished much to remove legal barriers to equality— freedom for slaves, racial integration in the military and in the schools, women's suffrage, gay rights;—but nothing has been done, or perhaps can be done (that's a policy forum question), about rising economic inequality. It has been so gradual as to have gone unnoticed, but the trend is now three decades old and it is not slowing down but accelerating. Is it a critical issue? As Tim Noah writes in his book *The Great Divergence*, (and I paraphrase), growing inequality is the single most threatening trend of modern times. It threatens opportunity, it destroys the American dream, and it puts the democracy at risk.

In the words of Nobel laureate economist Joseph Stiglitz, "we have a system that has been working overtime to move money from the bottom and the middle to the top, but the system is so inefficient that the gains to the top are far less than the losses to the middle and the bottom." (A few millions of dollars of bankers' bonuses are no match for the billions lost in home ownership.) "We are, in fact, paying a high price for our growing and out size inequality: not only slower growth and lower GDP but even more instability. And, this is not to say anything about the other prices we are paying: a weakened democracy, a diminished sense of fairness and justice, and even. . . a questioning of our sense of identity."

We don't have to scour far among the great humanists of literature and history to illuminate these issues. Victor Hugo just got nominated for an Academy Award by way of *Les*

Miserables; and there's always Jimmy Stewart fighting against Old Man Potter to keep his town from becoming Potterville; or battling Claude Rains in *Mr. Smith Goes to Washington*. Perhaps the humanities and the council can awaken us to the nature of this issue without accusations of class warfare or socialism, or worse. If any agency can do it, the Wyoming Humanities Council can.

Are there important things to do? I should say so! Is the council up to the challenge? You bet your life it is! It's an established, credible, respected institution on the verge of a new era—another rung on its tall ladder of success!

Nothing you haven't addressed—
Nothing you haven't done before—
Nothing you can't do now!

You're visioners, conveners, connectors, and optimists. I know you! I've worked with you! You fit the description that was nailed on the great door of the cathedral of Notre Dame in the eighteenth century "The world tomorrow will belong to those who bring it the greatest hope!"

You are the bringers of hope! I envy you your task, and I am excited to see the results!

Samuel Western

Samuel Western writes from Sheridan, where he has a heart-halting view of the Bighorn Mountains. The outdoors in all forms, literature, music, agriculture (farm to fork), community, and the human condition are his wellsprings. For twenty-five years, he wrote for *The Economist* and other publications. Now he concentrates on books, speaking, and teaching. His fiction is distilled and deals with core issues: faith, values, and the difficulties of meaningful change. His nonfiction attempts to address what historian Arnold Toynbee called the "deeper, slower movements that, in the end, make history." While he doesn't ignore social culture, he finds it's best attended to in small doses, although, to paraphrase Thoreau, nothing necessary offends him. He is a curious person.

From Democracy in Wyoming

It seems a bit of a stretch, comparing ancient Greece and Wyoming.

Rosy-fingered dawn, the wine-dark sea, and rows of olive trees bending in a soft wind. Put these idylls against high plains, cold, sagebrush, and wind socks so turgid that they look like they're stuffed with concrete.

The similarities remain, nonetheless. Yet we've got more complex political challenges than the residents of the historic Aegean.

Demos—the root word for democracy—has two meanings: village and people. Do not confuse this with a 1970s disco band. Village was the smallest political subdivision of the Athenian state. People meant the citizens of Athens. A modern analogue—although more inclusive—might be "We The People," the preamble to the United States Constitution.

Wyoming is a state of small villages. In 1950, Cheyenne, our largest city then and now, had just 32,000 people. Circa 2019, it's doubled in population. That's it. In that period, nearby Fort Collins's population grew by a factor of ten. Wyoming has just eight cities with more than ten thousand folks.

In these places, no one is a stranger. Cuss at someone at a county commissioner's meeting and, sure enough, you'll see them at the grocery store the next day.

Avoiding awkward meetings means walking the razor's edge: honesty and conviction on one side, diplomacy and civility on the other. It's not easy. But try avoiding it, especially the honesty, and learn the cost. The Greeks had two essentials when came to democracy: the permission to speak, regardless of station, and the freedom to speak your mind. If not raw honesty, why bother with debate, asked the orator Demosthenes. You end up no nearer to accomplishing any task than when you started.

Well, words can be weapons. Honesty for honesty's sake can border on vanity. A tongue of gall accomplishes little. That means choosing our words carefully.

Democracy depends on more than participation and what we say (and how we say it) in a roomful of people. It obliges adult civic choices when we're alone. Wyoming provides a lot of space where we can misbehave unseen. Most of us could dump used motor oil in the creek that runs behind our isolated two-acre lot.

But we do not. We've figured out that's bad for the commonwealth. Apparently, we have less compunction about our choices when sitting solo before our computer or fiddling with our smartphone. Isolation grants us the fiction we can get away with actions without having to answer to their consequences.

That's a hallmark of totalitarian or autocratic societies:

they grant powerful individuals immunity from poor choices. We can occasionally get away with this responsibility vacuum in functioning democracies.

It would be easy to blame others for these shortcomings. Look in the mirror instead. Unlike in ancient Athens, a key adult freedom is the choices we make when we're alone, either working the keyboard or standing before a ballot box. There we execute one of democracy's most critical demands: refusing fuel to flamethrowers and autocrats. Without followers, a bully is nothing. They're just out there on the prairie, yipping their lonely anthem, hoping for attention.

Bottom line: don't let fear drive the democratic process. Projecting catastrophe is a venerable and reliable agency. Its chief ally is the conviction is that unless we hurl verbal bombs, our opinion won't matter; that we can calm our anxieties by anonymous trolling; that things are so out of control that we require a strongman at the helm.

These are work-avoidance schemes. Democracy is face-to-face, side-by-side, and making brave choices when nobody's looking.

Phil Roberts

Phil Roberts is Professor of History Emeritus, University of Wyoming, where he has been on the faculty since 1990. He specializes in the history of Wyoming and the American West, legal, and environmental and natural resources history. He holds a Ph.D. in history from the University of Washington (1990) and the J.D. in law from the University of Wyoming (1977).

From "Civility in Politics: Wyoming's Mixed Rocord"

Civility in Wyoming, particularly with respect to politics and public affairs, has been as much honored in the breech as in practice. From territorial days, character assassination of political rivals was as commonplace in Wyoming as it was elsewhere in the nation. Some of the most venomous attacks came from the pages of newspapers. Nearly every Wyoming town had two newspapers—one, Republican; the other, Democratic. Political patronage determined where the primary source of revenues for papers in those days—legal advertising—would be placed. Winning was paramount to financial survival. With respect to national campaigns, the presidential winner determined who kept every post office job in the country and who remained as public land commissioner or territorial officer, down to the lowest-paid court clerk. After federal civil service reform removed much of the partisanship from career positions in federal service, in Wyoming, all agency employees until after World War II were subject to dismissal when a new governor took office. With the stakes so high, it is little wonder that the heat of political campaigning would often descend into incidents of appalling incivility. Still, in most cases, the "victory" frequently went to those maintaining the high road.

But political rivalry wasn't always restricted to Republicans versus Democrats. One of the most celebrated political feuds in the state's history involved two lifelong Republicans—two men known as the "grand old men of Wyoming politics" who had worked together closely to gain statehood for Wyoming—Francis E. Warren and Joseph M. Carey. In 1892, in the wake of the Johnson County War in which both Warren and Carey were implicated, Warren's two-year term in the United States Senate expired. US Senators were chosen by the legislatures, and Wyoming's newly elected members deadlocked on selections of a Warren replacement. Carey was Wyoming's only US Senator, but his term was to expire in 1894. It was apparent that the Wyoming legislature would no longer tolerate having two senators from Cheyenne. Consequently, Warren worked behind the scenes to convince legislators to dump Carey and, instead, send an Evanston man in his place while also naming Warren to the vacant seat. When Carey returned from Washington to the state capitol, he assumed he would be accepting re-nomination. Instead, he was humiliated when not one legislator cast a ballot for him.

Carey, rejected for the gubernatorial nomination by Republicans in 1910, gained the nomination from the Democrats and went on to win in the fall election. One of his first acts as governor was to establish primary elections, removing party nominations from closed conventions and backroom deals. In essence, some good did arise from the incivility.

Despite such incidents, Wyoming politics also had its moments when the debates over public issues were strenuous, but rivals respected each other's rights to disagree while respecting them as individuals. One example comes from the 1998 gubernatorial primary campaign. Jim Geringer, the incumbent governor, might have sat in his office in Cheyenne, shunning participation in public forums with his four opponents (one Republican and three Democrats). Instead, he came to public forums featuring all five candidates. Just before one of the major "debates" on Wyoming Public Television, Geringer and a staff member stopped at Wendy's for a quick lunch. A candidate from the other party had just come in, too, and after exchanging pleasantries at the counter, the two men and their respective staff members had lunch together in the restaurant, both of them greeting well-wishers who came by and introducing those that the other did not know. The incident wasn't isolated. In another case, a political rival called an opponent, asking which direction he was driving to be at a party forum in Rock Springs that next day. "Hey, my car is broken down," he said. "Would you mind if I hitchhiked with you? I could get down to Rawlins if you could pick me up at McDonald's down there." The two. . . drove together to Rock Springs where they hotly debated their respective views. And, after saying their "goodbyes," left together as they'd come.

One could point to contemporary examples that would mirror the vicious newspaper attacks of the nineteenth century, but one also could point to today's incidents of rivals "riding circuit" together, just as Lincoln and his opponents did on the Illinois frontier. Democracy and the political scene in Wyoming has survived the incivilities, but it has been from the debates over ideas, not the personal attacks, that have built community and moved us toward American goals of freedom and equality.

Marko Ruble

Marko Ruble is a graduate of the University of Wyoming and a former student in Pete Simpson's class, "Wyoming's Political Identity." Marko is a founding partner of A&R Trading, LLC, an import and export management services company. He resides in Cody, Wyoming with his wife, Lindsay, and two sons.

From Hamburgers in Jeffrey City

So, I sit down, and of course there's a guy bellied up to the bar and Fox News is on the TV. Yet to each their own. I just want to eat my burger and wonder what things would be like in Jeffrey City when the US energy demands make it worthwhile to go after uranium in the hills around the town again. And I'm down to the last few bites of my burger and the ketchup is starting to squeeze out from underneath the bun, as always happens when I eat a burger, which takes some concentration to keep it from dribbling onto my clothes. Mind you, I would be happy sitting there eating and wondering about this town which has a look of post-apocalypse when the guy at the bar wants to make friends.

Small talk ensues, and before I know it we are talking politics. I'm a poli sci major, and he asked what I did in school

The iconic Top Hat Motel sign in Jeffrey City is recognized throughout the state. The uranium mining boomtown established around 1957 went bust when the mine shut down in 1982 and 95% of its population left.

PHOTO BY LELAND RUCKER

and what on earth I planned to do with a poli sci degree. "Hopefully not much," I said. "Of course that depends on how good it pays." And then, boom! He laid it out on my table. The time for concentrating on not getting ketchup on my pants came.

"Them sons-a-bitches out there in Washington makin' their deals with liberals and lobbyists and tellin' us what to do all the time. I swear to Christ they should all be shot."

Damn it! It would be so much easier for me to say "yep" and go on, but I can't ignore the logic gene switching on in my DNA. It's time to chat.

"Would you be the one pulling the trigger?" I ask.

"Hell yeah, but I wouldn't be the only one."

"Is there a lot of people out here who feel this way?"

"God damn right there is," he says.

"But, this is a ghost town; nobody lives here."

"Well, I know people around this state."

The conversation could take a turn right into Fort Poordecisionton if not played right, so I ask him: "What's the first three digits of your social security number?"

"Five-two-zero, why?"

There's a reason this guy lives here. He's been screwed by people before, and there is a trust issue that will never be resolved by anything except living out here by uranium mines, sage brush, and the Sweetwater River.

"Just wondering if you're from Wyoming. And, you are. Where abouts did you grow up?"

"Rawlins," he says gruffly—the last of his beer foam caught on his mustache.

"You ever heard of Jay's Drive-In?"

"You kiddin' me? I used to go there all the time. They had the best burgers."

"Yeah, that was my mom's family's business. They had another restaurant over in Rock Springs, too."

Democracy Under Construction

"I'll be damned, you're a Santich?"

"No, a Ruble. My mom was Peggy Santich, but she married a guy with the last name Ruble."

"S..t, I went to school with yer mom. I always had a thing for her," he says.

Things could have gotten messy. It would have been easy to play devil's advocate and proclaim my bleeding heart liberalism, but it seems that would be about as productive as flickin' rattlesnakes just to see if it can be done. But, this conversation is part of Wyoming's political identity. The guy is ready to declare a call to arms against the federal government if enough people stand by him, but since that's not going to happen any time soon, we both realize there is a connection between us, and for him it involves having a school-age crush on my mother, and the best burgers he's ever had.

By the way, I don't remember if I got any ketchup on my clothes. I don't even remember if I finished the burger.

Anyway, the moral of the story: Wyoming is a small world, and here we are living in it. In a ghost town one can make a connection with a person one click shy of being a hermit. In essence, citizens of Wyoming can't get too mad at too many people for too long because there just aren't that many people to be mad at if indeed one wants to still be a part of Wyoming society. And, it's also a fixture of that glaring tenet of Wyoming's political identity: independence. A truly independent person will respect another's argument. It's inherent in the ability for one to call oneself independent. I love this place.

Grace Raymond Hebard

July 2, 1861 - October 1936

Grace Hebard served as a University of Wyoming professor for 28 years and was a prominent Wyoming historian. She was the first woman admitted to the Wyoming State Bar Association and admitted to practice before the Wyoming Supreme Court. Hebard was active in Wyoming political life, organizing historical associations, participating in the local and national suffragist movement, lobbying for child-welfare laws, serving as a Red Cross volunteer, and selling war bonds during WWI.

From Washakie: An Account of Indian Resistance of the Covered Wagon and Union Pacific Railroad Invasions of Their Territory (1930)

One of the reports prepared by Governor [John Wesley] Hoyt gives a graphic description of the gracious reception accorded him upon meeting the great chief of the Shoshones:

[Hoyt writes,] "I was cordially received by Chief Washakie and thirty of his chief men, all rising, and with smiles and words of welcome in concert, which I could not quite, and yet did sufficiently, understand…

"The chief, rising slowly, then delivered himself of a speech as remarkable for its power and pathos as any ever heard."

"We are right glad, sir," [Washakie] said, "that you have so bravely and kindly come among us. I shall, indeed, speak to you freely of the many wrongs we have suffered at the hands of the white man. They are things to be noted and remembered. But I cannot hope to express to you the half that is in our hearts. They are too full for words.

"Disappointment; then a deep sadness; then a grief inexpressible; then, at times, a bitterness that makes us think of the rifle, the knife, and the tomahawk, and kindles in our hearts the fires of desperation – that, sir, is the story of our experience, of our wretched lives.

"The white man, who possesses this whole vast country from sea to sea, who roams over it at pleasure, and lives where he likes, cannot know the cramp we feel in this little spot, with the undying remembrance of the fact, which you know as well as we, that every foot of what you proudly call America, not very long ago belonged to the red man. The Great Spirit gave it to us. There was room enough for all his many tribes, and all were happy in their freedom. But the white man had, in ways we know not of, learned some things we had not learned; among them, how to make superior tools and terrible weapons, better for war than bows and arrows; and there seemed no end to the hordes of men that followed them from other lands beyond the sea.

"And so, at last, our fathers were steadily driven out, or killed, and we, their sons, but sorry remnants of our tribes once mighty, are cornered in little spots of the earth all ours of right – cornered like guilty prisoners, and watched by men with guns, who are more than anxious to kill us off.

"Nor is this all. The white man's government promised us that if we, the Shoshones, would be content with the little patch allowed us, it would keep us well supplied with everything necessary to comfortable living, and would see that no white man should cross our borders for our game, or for anything that is ours. *But it has not kept its word!* The white man kills our game, captures our furs, and sometimes feeds his herds upon our meadows. And your great and mighty government – Oh sir, I hesitate, for I cannot tell the half! It does not protect us in our rights. It leaves us without the promised seed, without tools for cultivating the land, without implements for harvesting our crops, without breeding animals better than ours, without the food we still lack, after all we can do, without the many comforts we cannot produce, without the schools we so much need for our children.

"I say again, *the government does not keep its word!* And so, after all we can get by cultivating the land, and by hunting and fishing, we are sometimes nearly starved, and go half naked, as you see us!

"Knowing all of this, do you wonder, sir, that we have fits of desperation and think to be avenged?"

Tom Rea

Tom Rea lives in Casper, Wyoming, where he is editor and co-founder, with the Wyoming State Historical Society, of WyoHistory.org. He worked for many years in the newspaper business, and his books include *Bone Wars: The Excavation and Celebrity of Andrew Carnegie's Dinosaur* (University of Pittsburgh Press, 2001, 2004), *Devil's Gate: Owning the Land, Owning the Story* (University of Oklahoma Press, 2006, 2012), *The Hole in the Wall Ranch: A History* (Pronghorn Press, 2010).

From "Right Choice, Wrong Reasons: Wyoming Women Win the Right to Vote"

Thanks in part to an uneducated Virginian who held many of the racist views of his time, Wyoming Territory became the first government in the world to guarantee women the right to vote.

William Bright was a saloonkeeper from South Pass City, a Gold Rush boomtown nearly as big as Cheyenne at the time. He had served in the Union Army all through the Civil War.

After the war, he and his young wife, Julia, moved to Salt Lake City. Gold was discovered in 1867 near South Pass, and Bright moved to South Pass City that summer. He made good money selling mining claims. The next spring, Julia Bright and the couple's baby son, William Jr., joined him there.

That was a presidential election year, and William Bright was a Democrat. During the Civil War, northern Democrats were unsure the killing was worth the cost and would have preferred a truce or compromise. After the war, Democrats continued to oppose full citizenship and voting rights for formerly enslaved people and for Blacks who had been more or less free already.

Congress, controlled by the Republicans, soon passed two new constitutional amendments. The Fourteenth Amendment guaranteed citizenship and full protection of the law to former slaves. The Fifteenth Amendment promised that no people could be denied the right to vote based on color or "previous condition of servitude." Both were soon ratified by the states and became law.

In May 1868, Democrats in South Pass City called a meeting to choose a delegate to the national convention, where the party would choose its presidential candidate. William Bright and sixteen other men signed a newspaper ad warning that only strong Democrats should attend—men who opposed votes for Black people and opposed the Radical Republicans who were running Congress. Bright chaired the meeting. That fact offers a glimpse of his political feelings—and probably his racial ones.

The next year, Bright opened a saloon on South Pass City's busiest corner—a good way to become well known. Bright may have been thinking of going into politics.

A new president, Ulysses S. Grant, a Republican, took office in March 1869. Soon he appointed Republicans to run the brand-new Wyoming Territory. These included Governor Joseph Campbell and Attorney General Joseph Carey; they arrived in May. Carey soon issued an official legal opinion that no one in the territory could be denied the right to vote based on race.

The first territory-wide election was held in September. Many Democrats, probably correctly, saw Carey's opinion as a move to make sure Wyoming's Black people voted Republican. To Campbell's chagrin, however, only Democrats were elected. The territory's new delegate to Congress was a Democrat, as were all twenty-two members of the new territorial legislature.

William Bright won a seat in the [Territorial] Council—the precursor to the Wyoming state senate. The other councilors elected him president of the [Territorial] Council, which meant he would chair the meetings and control the flow of bills.

When the legislature convened in Cheyenne in October, the legislators all seem to have been interested in women's rights. They passed laws guaranteeing women and men teachers equal pay and guaranteeing married women property rights separate from their husbands.

The idea of votes for women was not new in American politics. Before the Civil War, abolitionists and women's rights advocates were strong allies. After the war, however, Republicans put women's rights on the back burner, and many women felt betrayed.

Meanwhile, Washington and Nebraska territories in the 1850s tried and failed to give women the vote, two national efforts had failed after the Civil War, and early in 1869, Dakota Territory came within one vote of passing a woman's suffrage bill. Many of Wyoming's legislators came from places where the question had been often discussed.

Late in the legislative session, William Bright introduced a bill to give Wyoming women the right to vote.

First, lawmakers wanted good publicity to draw more settlers—especially women—to a territory where there were at the time six men for every woman. Second, legislators, all Democrats, hoped that once these women arrived, they would vote Democratic.

Third, these Democrats wanted to embarrass their Republican governor. Many assumed Campbell would veto the bill. His party championed the rights of ex-slaves, but given a chance to extend the vote to women, the legislators suspected, he wouldn't do it.

Fourth, many of the legislators believed strongly that if Blacks and Chinese were to have the vote, then women—especially white women—should have it, too. A Cheyenne newspaper reported this as "the clincher" argument. "Damn it," an unnamed legislator supposedly said, "if you are going to let the"—here he used extremely harsh terms for Black and Chinese—"vote, we will ring in the women, too."

Stories also circulated in later years that the whole thing had been a joke, a claim that goes against the fact that legislators spent a great deal of time debating the issue.

And finally, some lawmakers wanted to give the vote to women simply because it was the right thing to do. Bright was among this number, as well.

The bill passed the [Territorial] Council 6–2. The House amended it to raise the voting age for women from 18 to 21, then passed it 7–4. Campbell, after some days' thought, signed the bill December 10, 1869.

Later that month, Bright in South Pass City welcomed a congratulatory visit from John Morris and his wife, Esther Hobart Morris. John Morris later wrote a letter about their conversation to *The Revolution*, a national women's rights magazine. John Morris wrote that Bright was glad to see them, as they were among a very few people in town who favored the new law.

Early in 1870, Esther Morris was appointed justice of the peace, becoming the first woman ever to hold public office. In 1870 and 1871, women served on juries in Laramie.

In September 1870, women finally got the chance to vote in Wyoming Territory's second election. To the disgust of the Democrats who had handed them the vote, a great many voted Republican.

Two years later, Campbell vetoed a bill to repeal the 1869 law. The House overrode him, but the [Territorial] Council fell one vote short. The law was never challenged again. All women in the United States did not win the right to vote for nearly fifty more years.

In 1902, Bright was noticed in the audience at a national women's rights convention. Asked to speak about what had happened in Wyoming, he replied that the bill was not introduced "in fun." He said he supported the idea because he believed "his wife was as good as any man and better than convicts and idiots," the *Women's Tribune* reported. If he mentioned Black people at this point, or used a more derogatory term, the paper did not repeat it.

Perhaps the story shows that the right thing sometimes happens for a large, strange mix of reasons, many of them wrong. Or as John Morris wrote to *The Revolution*, "It is a fact that all great reforms take place, not where they are most needed, but in places where opposition is weakest; and then they spread. . . ."

Captain Larry V. Birleffi

April 17, 1918 - September 27, 2008

Larry Birleffi was born on April 17, 1918, in Hartville, Wyoming. He graduated from Sunrise High School and then the University of Wyoming in 1942, with a major in journalism, marrying Lois Sturtevant in 1944. They would eventually have three daughters, Lynn, Bobbie and Laurie.

Known as the Voice of the Wyoming Cowboys, Birleffi's career as a sportscaster and writer spans the history of broadcasting itself. He began as a sportswriter for the *Laramie Daily Boomerang*, moved into radio, and finally television. His voice and image have been seen and heard throughout the Rocky Mountain West and nationally. Ten years into his career, he was named Man of the Year in Wyoming. Twenty years into his career the governor proclaimed Larry Birleffi Day, and thirty years in, the University of Wyoming named the football stadium press box after him.

Birleffi served as a Captain in the US Army 92nd Infantry Division for four years during World War II, earning a Bronze Star as a Major. Headquartered in Fort Huachuca, Arizona, the 92nd Division was one of three Negro divisions in the U.S. Army. In 1944, Captain Birleffi was sent to Italy to continue his duties there. He served as the Public Information Officer and published the company newspaper. Aboard ship on his way to Italy, he kept a diary (published here courtesy of Bobbie and Lynn Birleffi).

From the personal diary of Larry Birleffi, entry titled:
October 14, 1944—Aboard Ship

Our first night in Naples we stayed aboard ship in the harbor all night. Past midnight I went topdeck. Across the bay, the dull lights of Naples could be seen. The moon cast a brilliant glow upon the waters, and the outline of the other ships in the semi-darkness cast shadows on the tranquil bay.

So this was Naples, there like a limp fighter hanging over the ropes. I thought of those miserable people begging for cigarettes in the Messina Straits. I had a lonely ache for my darling wife and daughter. Then I thought of Dad.

This was the country Dad left behind him when he was a boy of thirteen to come to America. This was an old story, but I never thought of it before as I did that night in the harbor

Larry Birleffi during WWII. Date Unknown. Photo courtesy of Bobbi and Lynn Birleffi

of Naples. I thought of the time he told me how he cried for several solid months, a homesick, lonely boy in America. Dad never told me much about his early life, or his people in Italy. I wondered now why I hadn't asked him more. All I knew was that he came from somewhere near Rome. Then I remembered the time Dad got that letter from Italy. I was a young kid then. It was the only letter I remember my father ever received from Italy. It came from a sister, I believe, informing him of his mother's death, with morbid pictures of the funeral procession. Dad didn't say much. I didn't see him all day. He closeted himself in his bedroom, I guess.

Democracy Under Construction

I thought of Dad, now back there at the mining town in Wyoming, brokenhearted, trying to start life over again after all these years. I knew Dad was brokenhearted; I could see through a stout front he had built within himself. I realized he changed since my older brother was killed in 1942. I realized, too, he would never be the same again. I knew Mom suffered too, but she found much solace in her religion. But it was different with Dad. He believed in God, but he was twisted up all inside. He was proud of Art as a bomber pilot. He would drive miles to see his son land his B-17. That's all he talked about at the mines. And when Art received his permanent commission and later became a squadron leader, he must have busted all the buttons on his vest. My brother's plane was known as the *Uncle Biff*. Dad wanted to know why they call it that and I explained how Art as a squadron leader contracted the name uncle and the name Biff was a natural short for such a name as Birleffi. He was quite proud of that too. But everything has changed now, and I knew Dad was living on memories.

Yes, he had so much to be proud of. He had given both my brother and me a college education: Art's in civil engineering and mine in what might be called journalism. Dad always thought that suited me perfectly, because I was always talkative and had lots of "imagination." He had another name for it in Italian.

I wasn't home then, but I thought of the many days of deep humility Dad must have suffered to himself when Italy slugged France in the back and then went with Germany of how he took all jibes good-naturedly.

I knew Dad was ashamed of his people and former country. He never talked about it, but it wasn't necessary. I thought of the sonofabitch who had sent my father an anonymous note in the early days of the war, with dire notes for firing one of the men at the Mines and then signed it "An American." Dad had given much of his time on the draft board, and I knew he had sunk just about all the insurance money Art had left in war bonds. I'd like that guy that signed his name as an "American" to read this someday, although I know Dad wouldn't like it, because he just laughed at the note.

Dad was never a foreigner to me, he was always America. For almost forty years now he has been a reputable citizen. But it wasn't only that. I don't like flag waving and sentimentalities, but he is democracy to me. I've heard all sorts of definitions of democracy and have made attempts to define it myself. I always thought of Dad and his case and the thousands of experiences like it, where men came to America, raised families, and worked themselves to comfortable incomes. This is democracy.

Worn out as the story may be, to me this will always be a true democracy. I shall always love America for it. I shall always be willing to fight for it, as my children will be and their children, because I realize now my dad instilled it within me. I had to return to the land from where he came to grasp it firmly, to hold it forever.

The lights of Naples across the bay appeared brighter now. The moon's glow on the placid waters seemed iridescent. I felt much better as I returned below deck and to my bunk.

Sam Mihara

Sam Mihara is a second-generation Japanese American. When World War II broke out, Sam and his family were forced to stay in the Heart Mountain Relocation Center in Northern Wyoming for three years. After the war, Sam graduated from U.C. Berkeley and UCLA graduate school with engineering degrees and became a rocket scientist with The Boeing Company. In 2018 he received the Paul A. Gagnon Prize from the National Council for History Education for his work lecturing about his imprisonment as a child.

From Blindsided: The Life and Times of Sam Mihara

I was at Boeing during the Cold War. Some of what I made was for civilians—satellites in space for mass communication and prototypes for the first cell phones. But other Boeing projects were aimed at strengthening our military defense, and I worked on those, too. As I bolstered the US arsenal, I never batted an eyelash.

By the time I was a professional engineer, the men who had sent me to Heart Mountain were in graves. I did feel resentment toward them, but to me, they didn't represent America. There was a new wave of politicians who had replaced the old guard: John F. Kennedy and Camelot took over the Oval Office, and with them came the promise of a more tolerant, open-minded American people. We were young again, and we would not let fear control us.

With new leaders and vision, the United States once again shone as a beacon of freedom, and I never felt torn about helping our government. I wanted my skills to help promote peace, and I wanted to personally contribute to our national security. My bitterness toward the United States had mostly vanished as the '50s became the '60s, which in turn became the

'70s. I refused to judge all of America as a generalized swath, like some officials had judged the Japanese years before.

Times were changing, and I let them.

That's not to say that rancor never itched at the corners of my mind. I felt wronged for decades, both by the men who had condemned me, and by some of the people of Wyoming who had looked at me like I was a criminal. After I left Heart Mountain in 1945, I didn't return to the state until the 1970s. I wanted nothing to do with its residents who hated me, who had denounced me with derogations and demanded I stay in a prison far from their doorsteps.

But that anger subsided, too. I learned I was wrong. Even the people of Wyoming could change after World War II hysteria lost its power, and my hatred for them was no more righteous than the hatred previous generations had felt for me. And so I let that go, too.

As the new millennium approached, wounds began to heal. The Cold War ended, and perestroika meant that tolerance spread to even the most intolerant parts of the world. Two presidents, Ronald Reagan and George H. W. Bush, apologized in writing to us for the horrors we faced during World War II, finally admitting the US government's misstep. Meanwhile, I grew older and wiser as I learned not to let my past dictate my present.

A few years ago, when we opened a learning center where Heart Mountain used to be, every store in Cody put up a sign, Welcome Japanese Americans. And so the wrongest of the wrongs had been righted, in its own way.

Still, Heart Mountain has a legacy—one that Americans too easily forget. One hundred twenty thousand Japanese living in the United States were forced to leave their homes for prisons they never deserved, but today, only a few of us are still here to remember. Our stories have not been told as often as others. And "Japanese internment" does not harbor the same psychological potency as other manmade tragedies like the Holocaust, partly because its history has faced an erasure while that of other similar victimhoods have been burnt into the collective memory.

I have forgiven America for what it did to my family, but I refuse to let it forget. Because once we decide to distance ourselves from a part of our past, it is too easy to repeat the mistakes that took us down a dangerous path before. Registries. Detention centers. Racism. Religious segregation. They still exist here in the United States, and their victims still suffer.

There is another nine-year-old boy somewhere in America right now. He has spent years in detention because he and his immigrant family are unwanted by our government—by our country. As he stares at the white walls, he has learned to adapt to a new normal, though every day he longs to leave what lies behind his fence.

He is me. And you can save us.

Rodger McDaniel

Rodger McDaniel is a former Wyoming legislator (1971-1981). He was the Democratic Party nominee for the United State Senate in 1982. Rodger received a law degree from the University of Wyoming and a Master of Divinity degree from the Iliff School of Theology. He was the director of Habitat for Humanity operations in Nicaragua in 1991-1992. Rodger is the pastor at Highlands Presbyterian Church in Cheyenne, Wyoming where he lives with his wife Patricia.

From Dying for Joe McCarthy's Sins:
The Suicide of Wyoming Senator Lester Hunt

Joe McCarthy's Cold War witch hunts targeted people with same-sex attractions as much, maybe more than those with Communist sympathies. The rationale for the witch hunts and the laws criminalizing sexual acts between consenting gay and lesbian adults was a claim that homosexuals were security risks. It was said they could be easily blackmailed into giving up America's secrets. But the laws enacted in the late 1940s and early '50s to prevent that from happening had an unintended consequence. . . . The same demagogues who alleged homosexuals were subject to being blackmailed were, themselves, the perpetrators of one of the vilest blackmails in American political history.

The Lester Hunt story is as old as the story of Job of the Bible, a story constructed around a mythological wager. God lays a bet that good people will hold onto their beliefs in spite of being plagued with undeserved suffering. Satan calls God's bluff. They both double down on the life of Job. Job was unlike the rest of us. God said Job was "blameless and upright." Lester Hunt may not have reached that standard, although one of his colleagues eulogized Hunt, "He was wholly without guilt." There was never a hint of personal scandal in his personal or political life for the first sixty-one of his years. He was quite simply an honest, decent human being, whose suffering, like Job's, was undeserved.

Our lives are bookended between two dates—that of our birth and that of our death, dates separated by a small dash. For Hunt, the dash was nearly sixty-two years long. Yet the darkness of the last few hours had no beginning and no end. People who choose when to die are seldom able to place those last hours in the broader context of their lives no matter how well lived. The time from birth to death is compressed, made infinitely smaller than one's life, crystallized into that one moment.

It is not surprising that most of what is remembered of Lester Hunt is about that moment. Hunt's death was, in important ways, a metaphor for the times. Hunt's last hours were a part of the horror of the McCarthy years, the end of which may well have been hastened by Hunt's suicide.

Knowing how his life ends casts a shadow over the entire story, a shadow so dark as to sometimes eclipse the fascinating and engaged life Hunt led prior to those last few moments. Lester Hunt's life is a far more sustaining metaphor than was his death. The nefarious conduct of some of his Senate colleagues leading Hunt to choose death deserves to be condemned by exposure. The truth about his death should be told. But, it is not possible to understand his death without knowing more about his life. Perhaps in those last few hours, Hunt was overcome with a sense that the meaning of a lifetime of public service, loyalty to his family and his country, had been lost to the plans of a few villains. Those last hours may have seemed so dark that Lester Hunt was unable to see how bright a light his life had cast.

Perhaps in those last few hours, Lester Hunt made peace with the idea that there is something bigger to life than our few days on this earth. Lester Hunt had a deeper sense of purpose, what Joseph Campbell called "the mythologically inspired life." "The real heroes among us," Campbell said, "know when and to what to surrender. More than 2300 years earlier, Socrates took his own life. The great philosopher was accused of refusing to recognize the gods recognized by the state." It was the same charge leveled against Lester Hunt. For Socrates, it was the age of Apollo. For Hunt, it was the age of Joe McCarthy.

Fate had it that Lester Hunt's days in the United States Senate overlapped McCarthy's reign of terror. As Hunt arrived in Washington, McCarthy was beginning his melodramatic career as an unprincipled demagogue. Within days after Hunt's death, McCarthy was discredited. He was abandoned, even by most of those whose political careers had benefited from the drafting effect created by allowing him to run at the head of their pack.

Hunt refused to worship the gods of fear unleashed by McCarthy and his fellow travelers, gods who ruled over American politics, seeking to destroy the lives of good and decent people like the Wyoming senator. A century before Hunt came to Washington, a southern colleague who was unhappy with Missouri senator Thomas Hart Benton's refusal to support slavery confronted him on the floor. Senator Henry Foote of Mississippi "whipped out a pistol and pointed it at Benton, who dramatically threw open his coat and cried, 'I have no pistol. Let him fire, let the assassin fire!'" Not since had a Senator shown such courage in the face of a wanton attack as did Lester Hunt in the face of his character assassins.

When Socrates was convicted, he quietly acquiesced. He agreed to end his life by drinking poison. "I understand," he said. "I understand." History has been more kind to Socrates than to his accusers just as history will be more kind to Hunt than to his. As night fell on that sunny June morning, Lester

Hunt may well have said something similar to the last words of the Greek philosopher. "I understand."

Mythological heroes often leave everything familiar, go to a new land, and achieve extraordinary success. Lester Hunt was such a figure. As a young man with immeasurable optimism, he hopped a train and left behind everything familiar to begin life anew in Lander, a small Wyoming frontier town in the middle of nowhere. At first his new fellow townsfolk simply wanted him to come and play baseball for their small town team. In a few short years, they chose him to serve in high public office. Lester Hunt's story should have been a story of how hard work, decency, and honesty are rewarded. It would have been if not for the last year of his life. Lester Hunt's story will end violently. It is not the ending you might anticipate when walking through Hunt's early years in Illinois, watching him play baseball, excelling in school, and preparing for the extraordinary life ahead.

All of which bring us back to Socrates and the last words he spoke as he drank the poison. "We can and must pray to the gods that our sojourn on earth will continue happy beyond the grave. This is my prayer, and may it come to pass." The stories of real-life heroes do not often have happy endings. "For the Greeks, such a resolution (a happy ending) made for a comedy, whether it was funny or not, in contrast to a tragedy, which ended with a negative resolution," author Jack Hart has written. Lester Hunt's life story is not a Greek comedy. It's an American tragedy. Though it is without the happy ending he deserved and we might prefer, it should be told so that, as Socrates prayed, his "sojourn on earth will continue happy beyond the grave."

I have been asked frequently why I chose to write about Lester Hunt. It's a reasonable question given that no one has written about so many of the great political personalities of the state's history. Indeed, how unfortunate it is that the shelves of the public libraries across the state have so few books about the rich political history of Wyoming. So, I am asked, "Why Lester Hunt?"

I grew up in Wyoming. In high school and college, I took yearlong courses on Wyoming history. I devoted many of my years to politics, serving ten years in the state legislature and running as the Democratic Party nominee for the US Senate. Yet, I never heard the story of the suicide of one of Wyoming's United States senators. Dr. T. A. Larson wrote the textbook most widely used in Wyoming history courses. Dr. Larson's book simply says, "On June 19, 1954, Senator Lester C. Hunt, overwhelmed by political and personal problems, committed suicide." Dr. Larson wrote nothing more about the "political and personal problems" that overwhelmed Hunt. There is a fascinating story about why Larson left it at that. When I learned the nature of those problems, I wanted to tell the story.

There is another reason. Americans need to know this story, not only for the sake of Lester Hunt and his family, but for the realization it carries that the current lack of civility in the public arena is dangerous and that it has longer roots than we might think. Joe McCarthy is a long time dead and gone but his heirs are alive and well. The ruthless tactics honed by McCarthy and others named in this book continue to be a part of American politics. Today those who use such tactics benefit from having a twenty-four hour-a-day, seven-days-a-week news cycle, complete with entire radio and television networks dedicated to stretching and denying the truth in order to accomplish questionable ends.

McCarthy and the others would not have chosen the path they chose unless it worked for them and achieved their selfish ends. It continues to work today because a lazy, ill-informed electorate is willing to abdicate its responsibility to the agenda of others. If Lester Hunt's story had been told honestly in 1954, perhaps Americans would have been shocked into taking responsibility for the way in which their vote produced that outcome. It is difficult to imagine what it might take today to change the current ugly course of American discourse. It is, unfortunately, equally difficult to imagine that any democracy can survive this course.

These pages tell of Lester Hunt's ordeal because Americans must wrestle with the fact that the incivility we bemoan today started long ago and has become so much an accepted part of politics as to endanger the very survival of the republic. During the memorial service the Senate conducted for Hunt, "Big Ed" Johnson of Colorado said of his dead colleague, "Lester Hunt was a warm-hearted friendly soul. In his beloved Wyoming he respected and loved everyone, and everyone respected and loved him. Politics to him, as was his religion, was based on warm friendship, courtesy, kindness, gentleness, and goodwill toward all men."

We should all long for another day when public servants earn such a eulogy.

Clifford A. Bullock

Clifford Bullock earned his master of arts degree from the University of Wyoming in history. His article first appeared in the *Wyoming History Journal* volume 68 in 1996 as he examined the spread of the Black protests throughout the then-constituted Western Athletic Conference, when he and the other football players were summarily dismissed from the team leading to protests around the country.

From "Fired by Conscience"

The Wyoming football team was talented, successful, and a source of pride to the Equality State. The team had won an unprecedented three consecutive WAC football championships, and fans anticipated a fourth. During much of the decade, the Wyoming Cowboy football team was almost always among the nation's leaders. . . Prior to the 1969 season, the team had gone to the Sun Bowl and the Sugar Bowl. . . Ardent Wyoming fans expected another major bowl bid. Many Wyoming supporters envisioned an undefeated season while the university made plans to expand War Memorial Stadium to accommodate increased fan support. Fourteen Black football players were key to the team's success. . . These Blacks, along with a talented group of Whites, created a potent WAC football power. [But] many fans and boosters in Wyoming felt the team's success was attributable to head football coach Lloyd Eaton. . . Eaton was named WAC Coach of the Year in 1966 and 1967. . . [and] was reportedly "being considered" as a leading contender for the University of Pittsburgh head coaching job. . . Eaton. . . was regarded as a strict disciplinarian [and]. . . [he] believed team discipline to be a critical element in generating successful teams and quality athletes. He believed in the traditional, military-styled discipline of authoritarian athletics, even as Blacks around the country rebelled against its constraints. Part of Eaton's steps to establish discipline proved to be a key in the ensuing controversy. He forbade his players to be seen together in groups or to participate in any demonstration or protest. . . Just before the national Moratorium Day protests opposing United States involvement in Vietnam, on October 15, 1969, he reminded his players again. . . The fact there had been no protests to that date did not signify campus life in predominantly White Wyoming was without problems for Black athletes. . . [O]ne of the Cowboys' fourteen Black football players. . . left school for two years of military service when Coach Eaton opposed his marriage to a White woman. . . Black players endured racial slurs around the campus, in Laramie, and on the football field. Whatever grievances the Wyoming Blacks had were not publicly acknowledged as the team remained unbeaten and Bowl-bound.

On Moratorium Day, October 15, 1969, the newly formed Black Student Alliance of the University of Wyoming. . . delivered a letter to university officials. The letter referred to the racial policies of the LDS [Latter Day Saints] Church and BYU [Brigham Young University]. Included was a suggestion that players and students protest against BYU during the game scheduled in Laramie on October 18. . . Despite their coach's warning, the Black players met and decided they wanted to discuss with their coach what they felt to be a matter of conscience. On October 17, they walked to the athletic complex. They were in street clothes and wore black armbands to show Coach Eaton how they might protest. The coach requested that the group be seated in the bleachers at the field house. In the presence of two assistant coaches, Eaton called the Blacks "rabble rousers" who could no longer be supported by taxpayer money. . . Eaton then revoked their scholarships and dismissed them from the team. The calm on the Laramie campus vanished as the dismissals prompted a

battery of meetings involving the university president, the governor, the trustees, and the athletes themselves. In a vote of 17–1, it issued a statement condemning Eaton's actions, calling for a forum to discuss the rights of athletes as students. The senate also threatened to withhold student money from the athletic department. During the BYU game, picketers marched outside the stadium and the Black athletes were booed by the crowd when they took seats in the student section. During the game,

Former University of Wyoming Cowboys wide receiver John Griffin, left, and offensive lineman Mel Hamilton stand next to the Black 14 statue located in the student union of the University of Wyoming.

ANDY CARPENEAN, *LARAMIE BOOMERANG*

a large Confederate flag was displayed by a student at the top of the bleacher area. . . [T]he crowd chanted cheers for Eaton, confirming observers' feelings that Eaton was more popular than both [University of Wyoming] President Carlson and Governor Hathaway. . . Still, many students and faculty attended meetings and began petitions supporting the fourteen student athletes and calling for a reversal of the dismissals. The[se] groups focused on the issues of students' rights, academic freedom, the power of the athletic department, and free expression. . .

On October 23, 1969, President Carlson and Coach Eaton held a press conference and announced an immediate change in Eaton's rule regarding protests. This policy change would not affect, however, the Blacks already dismissed. It was at this press conference that *Sports Illustrated* reported that President Carlson admitted that at Wyoming, football was more important than civil rights.

Jess Fahlsing

Jess Fahlsing is originally from Rock Springs but now calls Laramie home. In 2019, Jess graduated from the University of Wyoming with bachelor's degrees in gender and women's studies and psychology. They received the Rosemarie Martha Spitaleri and Tobin Memorial Outstanding Graduate award, a recognition based on their scholarship, leadership, and contribution to service. Jess has planned community-oriented events, such as Laramie PrideFest, and is on the board of Wyoming Equality, the only statewide LGBTQ advocacy group. They are passionate about building connections and coalitions and, increasingly, intersectional activism. But Jess's heart remains where the journey began: with the Shepard Symposium on Social Justice, as cochair of Matthew Shepard's twentieth memorial. In their spare time, Jess like to travel, explore, spend time with friends, mountain bike, and enjoy the world's beauty. Jess's writing reflects love and hope, and the togetherness and community that have supported all they have accomplished.

From "To Matthew"

I grew up in the desert of Rock Springs, Wyoming. My body is meant for the wide open spaces. My heart is in the dust that would stick to my skin as I biked under wide blue skies, skin still vulnerable to being torn by rocks and by wrecking, even with the sunscreen. I think of the gears and chains of my bike, of mining into the earth. I think of my dad, who works for Jim Bridger power plant. I think of the height of the smoke stacks. I think of fossils, left from when the land was an ocean, and how my mom's dad collected rocks. I think of the college where she works, how it displays bones and fossils and taxidermied animals. I used to weigh my pack down with fossils, collecting them on my bike rides.

A little over twenty years ago, it was a mountain biker who found Matthew Shepard.

Sometimes all I want to do is just hop on my bike, and follow the path that came before me.

Other times, I cannot bring myself to confront both the joy of my bike and the trauma connected to it. With Matthew Shepard, we have focused so much on that loss and trauma. As an activist who lives in Laramie, I constantly come up against a sense of guilt if I take the time to simply exist. I am often brought back to a quote by Hannah Gadsby in her comedy special *Nanette*: "I identify as tired. Just tired." Like Hannah, I identify as tired and queer, along with non-binary, white, and disabled.

"You learn from the part of the story that you focus on," she also says. Too often, I focus on the losses I experienced, growing up queer in an old mining town that did not recognize my existence. . . and all that I have gained moving to Laramie, even as it is the town wherein Matt was murdered.

I was told to watch Hannah's special when walking in the prairie with a friend whom I met through various queer-centered spheres in my life. A friend, who I listened to as she talked about Matt Shepard and the pain the community of Laramie experiences surrounding his murder, a pain that is not often soothed by the university, a pain that perhaps, sometimes, we over-focus on. I held space for her, as I was in so much pain in my own life at that time. The cycle ebbs and flows, in a way that is not linear.

Many queer people's first thought upon hearing "Wyoming" is Matthew Shepard. While I do not blame them, I think of the difference that it has made for me to come to Laramie from Rock Springs. I think of the ways in which I almost did not survive the town that had no visible queer spaces, that erased my existence like deep ruts carved into the desert land from rain. I think of my mental illnesses that stemmed from such erasure. Yet I also try to think of the rainbow and trans flags that we have displayed for pride celebrations in Laramie, and how one person who recently joined our planning committee for Laramie PrideFest told me, "I was very nervous before moving to Laramie, but then I saw the flags displayed all over town last June. I felt a whole lot better after that."

I do not own Matthew's story. Whenever I am asked to write or to speak about him, there is a moment of impostor syndrome, behind which hides my exhaustion. The weight can become too much, and I fear that we idolize him in some ways. Matt was a person; more than a legacy. More than trauma. I often carry him with me, and I cannot forget that queer lives and bodies are targeted today, across the country, across the world. In Matthew's legacy lies a representation of queer bodies that have been harmed, erased, murdered, silenced, including transwomen of color, whose average life expectancy in this country is currently thirty-five years.

My own body remembers the fear that I carry. In my tense muscles is the caution that I cradle so closely. I have learned to ignore calls from trucks, and the sometime stares from when I walk in downtown Laramie. When people gasp to see me in certain gendered restrooms. When I am near a partner. When I am near my queer and beloved friends. My body responds to fear and to love, both. Sometimes, it is easy to forget the difference, especially when my own anger factors in.

There is a reason—or, perhaps a few—that I had remained alone and single for so damn long.

When faced with my loneliness or emptiness of the Wyoming lands, I often prefer to instead think about the time that Dennis Shepard tied my tie; or when Judy Shepard hugged me at a dinner where she received her honorary degree and I was recognized as one of the two outstanding graduates at the University of Wyoming. I think of how I have always claimed again and again that the only reason I am where I am today is because of the people in my life. I think of how I have repeated "We are stronger together. Now, and always. We are more than our trauma. We are more than the worst that has happened to us."

I return to the questions, What does it mean to have grown up in the state where Matthew Shepard was murdered? What does it mean to have gone to college in the town where it happened?

Every day, it means to challenge myself to become more inclusive and more aware of the intersectional overlap of the identities within the queer community.

Some days, it means turning home early from a bike ride, my thoughts too much and the intensity of a place too stark.

Some days, it means standing in front of a crowd and speaking, when all I really want to do is run away into the mountains and remember what it is like to simply breathe; breathe, and not have to speak.

Some days, it means I forget to be afraid, and then I am reminded, and am left wondering why I should remember to be afraid in the first place.

Many days, it means finding the miracle of love every day, in both small and large moments. It means texting my mom whenever I am back from a bike ride with the words, "I love you." Remember this—tell the important people in your life how much you love them.

Increasingly these days, it also means not waking up alone. It means greeting the day with someone whose smile brings me joy, and with whom I can rest when the weight gets to be a bit too much. A queer body, safe next to mine as we weather the night's darkness together. Someone, who often goes biking with me.

You learn from the part of the story that you focus on.

It is a hard, exhausting, constant fight, and sometimes it is a fight that we lose; sometimes it is a fight that we forget why we are fighting, but it is a fight always focused and centered on togetherness and on love.

To Matthew. We miss you. We will keep missing you. We will always miss you.

To Matthew. To Wyoming. To love.

Jeffery A. Lockwood

Jeffery Lockwood is a professor of natural sciences and humanities in the Department of Philosophy and the Creative Writing Program at the University of Wyoming. He teaches environmental ethics, philosophy, and creative nonfiction writing. He is the author of *The Infested Mind: Why Humans Fear, Loathe, and Love Insects* and the coauthor of *Philosophical Foundations for the Practices of Ecology.*

From Behind the Carbon Curtain:
The Energy Industry, Political Censorship, and Free Speech

[Behind the Carbon Curtain] has told the stories of artists, scientists, and educators censored by the energy industry in collusion with the government. Perhaps some readers will be unsurprised, but I hope that many are disturbed, even outraged. If I've succeeded, these people will be wondering what's next. What can anyone in a small town or a large state or a massive nation do about the silencing of voices?

Let me start by saying I don't know. I'm not a social scientist or political activist. But from the stories in *Behind the Carbon Curtain*, it would appear that there are two structural defects that foster censorship in Wyoming. First, the hegemony of the energy industry is undoubtedly a contributing factor. A diversified economy would mitigate this concentration of power, but exactly how Wyoming can achieve this outcome is a decades-old puzzle that economists and political scientists with far greater mastery of such matters than my own understanding have yet to solve.

The second defect pertains to the connection between political elections and corporate money. And this is a challenge to our democratic government and capitalistic economy that is also beyond my realm of legitimate expertise—not to mention that it would be the subject of another book altogether. Social scientists might be able to find ways of disconnecting politics and business, but I suspect that the solutions will require great insight and nuance.

So what about the rest of us? I believe that grassroots resistance to the abuse of power complements higher-order structural corrections. The mechanisms of change are not an either-or proposition (national structures or local movements). Consider how protests in Ferguson, Missouri, and elsewhere are fueling national changes in policies. . . . I don't claim to know how movements arise and why they succeed. I suspect that such phenomena are much easier to explain after the fact than to predict in advance. That said, three elements of social action are worth considering. These insights may lack radical originality, but sometimes novelty is overrated.

First, with regard to free speech, nothing is likely to change—except for the worse—if we don't recognize that there is censorship. Those in power do not willingly give up their capacity to control material and social resources; the rich get richer in terms of money and influence, so share this book with friends and neighbors. But share your own story as well. I suspect that the practice of censorship is among the most challenging injustices to address. How do we raise our voices when the problem is that people are being silenced? If a person fears retribution, then speaking out is not an easy task. But it is incumbent on us to object in some way to whoever we think might listen. Maybe it is at the dinner table or during a coffee break or after Sunday service or in a Rotary Club meeting or through a letter to the editor. Say something.

Second, we should heed the wisdom of Margaret Mead, who said, "Never doubt that a small group of thoughtful, committed citizens can change the world. Indeed, it is the only thing that ever has." Massive protests on the mall of of Washington, DC, are great, but big changes often arise through the accumulation of small actions (hence, the notion of a tipping point in complex systems). I don't know if we can fix censorship in Wyoming without national legislation to stop corporations from effectively purchasing election results. But then, had the people of Ferguson, Missouri, waited for Black Lives Matter to become a national movement, they'd still be sitting quietly in their homes. We must begin to solve problems for which the solutions are yet to be imagined.

Third, as a university professor I'm ineluctably drawn to the power of education. I worry that young people don't grasp the nature or importance of free speech. Surveys by the First Amendment Center have been profoundly revealing—and worrying.

Although 47% of Americans name freedom of speech as the most important liberty (freedom of religion is next at 10%), 36% could not identify this or any other right as being guaranteed by the First Amendment. And in terms of the need for education, young people tend to more strongly agree that the Constitution goes too far with freedoms. While 47% of people eighteen to thirty years old agree that the First Amendment overreaches in the rights it guarantees, just 24% of those forty-six to sixty years old agree.

And when Americans are afraid, their tolerance of First Amendment rights declines even further. After the Boston Marathon bombing, there was sharp jump in the proportion of people who thought the First Amendment excessively protected our freedom. And after the September 11 attacks, about 40% favored restrictions on the academic freedom of professors to criticize government military policy during war.

Today, 63% of Americans rate the educational system as doing only a fair to poor job in teaching students about the First Amendment. Perhaps people are right. Knowledge that the US Constitution guarantees freedom of speech is trending downward. As the country becomes more diverse, free speech may erode further. African Americans and Hispanics are more likely to say that the First Amendment overreaches. Fifty-two percent of African Americans and 50% of Hispanics agree, while only 29% of whites agree that the First Amendment goes too far.

The task of educators is daunting. Perhaps students who read this book will be unperturbed: "What can you expect when you bite the hand that feeds you?" But I also worry that students will just be perplexed: "Don't private and public employers have the right to decide what their employees can say and write?" Maybe I'm being uncharitable, but remember the effect of fear on our tolerance for oppression. The fear of foreign attacks trumps our defense of free speech, and one has to imagine that economic fears—particularly given the misery of the Great Recession for young people seeking work—will have a corresponding effect. If we do not defend freedom in our classrooms, we may well lose liberty in our town, states, and nation.

There are three caveats for those wanting to take action in response to corporate-sponsored censorship by politicians and government agencies. First, be careful. No viable ethical system requires self-destruction. My job is secure, but this is not the case for most people, who are at-will employees. Heed the admonition of General George Patton to US troops in 1944: "No bastard ever won a war by dying for his country. He won it by making the other poor dumb bastard die for his country."

Second, be courageous. It is also true that no action is morally praiseworthy if one stands to lose nothing. Justice entails struggle, while remaining silent is safe. Of course, for some people, perhaps many, other demands on their lives make the risks of social action untenable. As Socrates recognized centuries ago, courage is profoundly contextual. Each person must decide what free speech is worth compared to the costs of speaking out. But as Marianne Williamson wrote, "Our deepest fear is not that we are inadequate. Our deepest fear is that we are powerful beyond measure."

My third caveat concerns the nature of commitment. In working toward a more just world, we often yearn for the completion of our task. We pin our hopes on success, on seeing the fruits of our labor. We aspire to make our town or state or nation into a place where people can express themselves without fear of retribution. But the work of social justice will never be done. That is the curse and the blessing of being human. It's a curse in that there is no completion of our labors, a blessing in that there shall always be meaningful work.

To know what we can do, to understand what the world needs of us, we must hear the muted voices of our neighbors, read the accounts of destroyed art and suppressed science, and listen for what can't be said in classrooms. But to sustain our work, we must look inside ourselves. There we shall find the understanding that world-making is self-making, that the endless labor of life is about repairing our own dignity. It is good to cultivate freedom, whether or not it fixes a broken democracy.

Terry Tempest Williams

An American writer, educator, conservationist, and activist born in 1955 within sight of Great Salt Lake, Terry Tempest Williams' writing is inspired by the American West and influenced by the arid landscape of Utah and its Mormon culture. Her work focuses on social and environmental justice from issues of ecology and protection of public lands and wildness, to women's health, to exploring our relationship to culture and nature.

In 2003, she co-founded the University of Utah's (UU) acclaimed Environmental Humanities master's degree program and received an honorary doctorate. She taught at UU for thirteen years. Currently, she is Writer-in-Residence at the Harvard Divinity School, where she teaches "Finding Beauty in a Broken World" and "Apocalyptic Grief and Radical Joy." She works with the Planetary Health Alliance and the Center for the Study of World Religions, establishing The Constellation Project where the sciences and spirituality are conjoined.

From The Open Space of Democracy

Democracy invites us to take risks. It asks that we vacate the comfortable seat of certitude, remain pliable, and act, ultimately, on behalf of the common good. Democracy's only agenda is that we participate and that the majority voice be honored. It doesn't matter whether an answer is right or wrong, only that ideas be heard and discussed openly.

We are nothing but whiners if we are not willing to put our concerns and convictions on the line with a willingness to honestly listen and learn something beyond our own assumptions. Something new might emerge through shared creativity. If we cannot do this, I fear we will be left talking with only like-minded people, spending our days mumbling in the circles of the mad. I recall the words of William Faulkner: "What do we stand to lose? Everything."

How we choose to support a living democracy will determine whether it will survive as the breathing heart of a republic or merely be preserved as a withered artifact of a cold and ruthless empire.

"Fear and silence and spiritual isolation must be fought today," wrote Albert Camus in his essay "Neither Victims nor Executioners" in 1946, one year after World War II ended. I believe his words are contemporary. We can ask ourselves within the context and specificity of our own lives, how fear can be transformed into courage, silence transformed into honest expression, and spiritual isolation quelled through a sense of community.

Politics may be a game of power and money to those who have it, but for those of us who don't, politics is the public vehicle by which we exercise our voices within a democratic society.

At the end of Camus's essay, he states, "He who bases his hopes on human nature is a fool, he who gives up in the face of circumstances is a coward. And henceforth, the only honorable course will be to stake everything on a formidable gamble: that words are more powerful than munitions."

To commence. To begin.

To comment. To discuss.

To commend. To praise and entrust.

To commit to the open space of democracy is to begin to make room for conversations that can move us toward a personal diplomacy. By personal diplomacy, I mean a flesh-and-blood encounter with public process that is not an abstraction but grounded in real time and space with people we have to face in our own hometowns. It's not altogether pleasant, and there is no guarantee as to the outcome. Boos

Democracy Under Construction

and cheers come in equal measure.

If we cannot engage in respectful listening, there can be no civil dialogue, and without civil dialogue, we the people will simply become bullies and brutes, deaf to the truth that we are standing on the edge of a political chasm that is beginning to crumble. We all stand to lose ground. Democracy is an insecure landscape.

Do we dare to step back—stretch—and create an arch of understanding?

Additional
Biographies

Susan B. Anthony

February 15, 1820 – March 13, 1906

Susan B. Anthony was an American women's rights activist and women's suffrage leader. Raised a Quaker and dedicated to social reform, Anthony cofounded the New York Women's State Temperance Society with Elizabeth Cady Stanton in 1852 and the abolitionist Women's Loyal National League a year later. She became the New York state agent for the American Anti-Slavery Society in 1856 and subsequently founded the newspaper *The Revolution* and organizations such as the American Equal Rights Association and the National Women's Suffrage Association. In 1878, Anthony and Stanton presented Congress with an amendment guaranteeing women the right to vote. It was ratified as the Nineteenth Amendment in 1920. Anthony was the first woman to appear on United States currency, on the 1979 dollar coins.

Dr. Scott Henkel

Dr. Scott Henkel is the director of the Wyoming Institute for Humanities Research at the University of Wyoming, where he is also an associate professor in the departments of English and African American and Diaspora Studies. He is a member of the Board of Directors of Wyoming Humanities. His book, *Direct Democracy: Collective Power, the Swarm, and the Literatures of the Americas*, won a 2018 C. L. R. James Award for Best Published Book for Academic or General Audiences from the Working-Class Studies Association.

Thomas Jefferson

April 13, 1743 – July 4, 1826

Thomas Jefferson was an American diplomat, architect, philosopher, lawyer, statesman, and Founder. He served as the country's second vice president (1797–1801) and the third president (1801–09). He was a primary author of the Declaration of Independence, and a lifetime proponent of democracy, republicanism—a form of representative government—and individual rights. His advocacy in these areas helped motivate American colonists to break free from the British monarchy. Jefferson was a slaveholder; recent scholarship has shown the ways his life and livelihood was marked by this fact and contradicts his positions on equality and democracy. Jefferson studied mathematics, horticulture, and mechanics in addition to architecture, law, philosophy, and several languages. Jefferson's one full-length book is *Notes on the State of Virginia*.

Chief Washakie

c. 1808 – February 20, 1900

Washakie was a prominent Shoshone chief widely celebrated for his battle prowess, peace efforts, and commitment to his people's welfare. Considered the head of the Eastern Shoshone by the United States after he led a group of Shoshone representatives to the council meetings of the 1851 Treaty of Fort Laramie, he went on to sign two more land treaties at Fort Bridger, Wyoming. A US Army outpost was named in his honor after he led General Cook's defeat of the Sioux; and upon his death, he was given a full military funeral service, the only Native American to receive such a service. Washakie is remembered by his many namesakes, from Wyoming's Washakie County to a World War II Liberty ship, and by multiple statues, across Wyoming and in the National Statuary Hall Collection.

References and
Suggested
Readings

Booker, George. "The Rules of Civility and Decent Behavior." *Tidings*, 15 Sep. 2009, tidings org/2009/09/15/the-rules-of-civility-and-decent behavior/.

Bowers, Carol L. "School Bells and Winchesters: The Sad Saga of Glendolene Myrtle Kimmel." *Readings in Wyoming History: Issues in the History of the Equality State*, edited by Phil Roberts, 4th ed., Skyline West Press / Wyoming Almanac, 2004, pp. 53-77.

Bullock, Clifford A. "Fired by Conscience: The Black 14 Incident at the University of Wyoming and Black Protest in the Western Athletic Conference, 1968–1970." *Readings in Wyoming History: Issues in the History of the Equality State*, edited by Phil Roberts, 4th ed., Skyline West Press / Wyoming Almanac, 2000, pp. 184-196.

Burgess, Guy, and Heidi Burgess. "The Meaning of Civility." Beyond Intractability, Dec. 2019, www.beyondintractability.org/essay/civility.

Carter, Stephen L. *Civility: Manners, Morals, and the Etiquette of Democracy*. Harper Perennial, 1999.

Cartledge, Paul. *Democracy*: A Life. Oxford UP, 2018.

Cole, Bruce, and Judith Martin. "Civility in a Democracy: A Conversation with Miss Manners." *Humanities* vol. 26, no. 1, 2005, pp. 4–8, 51–54.

Connolly, William E. *Pluralism*. Duke UP, 2005.

Dahnke, Cassandra, et al. *Reclaiming Civility in the Public Square: 10 Rules That Work*. WingSpan Press, 2007.

Daniels, Roger. *Prisoners Without Trial: Japanese Americans in World War II*. Hill and Wang, 1993.

Darr, Christopher R. "Adam Ferguson's Civil Society and the Rhetorical Functions of (In)Civility in United States Senate Debate." *Communication Quarterly,* vol. 59, no. 5, 2011, pp. 603–24.

"The Declaration of Independence of the United States." The U.S. National Archives and Records Administration. https://www.archives.gov/founding-docs/declaration-transcript

Dewey, John. *Democracy and Education.* 1916. Free Press, 1997.

Douglass, Frederick. "What, to the Slave, is the Fourth of July?" *Great Speeches by African Americans*, edited by James Daley, Dover Publications, 2006, pp. 13–34.

Ehrlich, Gretel. *The Solace of Open Spaces.* Penguin Books, 1986.

Emerson, Ralph Waldo. "Self Reliance." 1841. Essays. Library of America, 1983. pp. 259-282.

"Erosion of Civility Not Unique to Times." *Troy Record*, 23 Feb. 2010. Editorial.

Fineman, Howard. *The Thirteen American Arguments: Enduring Debates That Define and Inspire Our Country.* Random House, 2010.

Fixico, Donald. *Rethinking American Indian History.* U of New Mexico P, 1997.

Flood, Renee Sansom. *Lost Bird of Wounded Knee: Spirit of the Lakota.* Scribner, 1995.

"The Freedom to Read Statement." American Library Association, 26 Jul. 2006, http://www.ala.org/advocacy/intfreedom/freedomreadstatement.

Galston, William. *Liberal Purposes: Goods, Virtues, and Diversity in the Liberal State.* Cambridge UP, 1991.

Golway, Terry. "A Plea for Civility: 'Cheapening Political Discourse.'" *America: The National Catholic Weekly*, 24 Mar. 2008, www.americamagazine.org/issue/650/columns/plea-civility.

Hasselstrom, Linda M., et al., eds. *Crazy Woman Creek: Women Rewrite the American West.* Houghton Mifflin, 2004.

Hebard, Grace Raymond. *Washakie: An Account of Indian Resistance of the Covered Wagon and Union Pacific Railroad Invasions of Their Territory.* Arthur C. Clark, 1930.

Herbst, Susan. *Rude Democracy: Civility and Incivility in American Politics.* Temple UP, 2010.

Holbrook, David J. *The Native Path.* Wyoming State Department of Education, 2005.

---. *The Native Path Teaching Resource Guide.* Wyoming State Department of Education, 2005.

Hufsmith, George. *The Wyoming Lynching of Cattle Kate, 1889.* High Plains Press, 1993.

"In Praise of Civility." *Dallas Morning News*, 25 Feb. 2010, p. A16. Editorial.

Ishigo, Estelle. *Lone Heart Mountain.* 1972.

Jensen, Paul. *The State of Equality in the Equality State.* Pronghorn Press, 2009.

Jones, Nick. "Civility, Sincerity, and Ambiguity." *Alabama Humanities Review*, no. 1, 31 Mar. 2011, alahumanitiesreview.wordpress.com/2011/03/31/civility-sincerity-and-ambiguity/.

Hamilton, Alexander, et al. *The Federalist Papers*. 1787–88. Edited by Isaac Kramnick, Penguin Books, 1987.

Larson, T. A. *History of Wyoming*. 2nd ed., U of Nebraska P, 1990.

Levine, Peter. "Teaching and Learning Civility." *New Directions for Higher Education*, no. 152, 2010, pp. 11–17.

Lincoln, Abraham. Second Inaugural Address; endorsed by Lincoln, 10 Apr. 1865. The Abraham Lincoln Papers, Series 3, General Correspondence, 1837–97, Manuscript Division, Library of Congress, www.loc.gov/collections/abraham-lincoln-papers/.

Lockwood, Jeffrey A. *Behind the Carbon Curtain: The Energy Industry, Political Censorship, and Free Speech*. U of New Mexico P, 2017.

Loffreda, Beth. *Losing Matt Shepard: Life and Politics in the Aftermath of Anti-Gay Murder*. Columbia UP, 2000.

Mackey, Mike, ed. *The Equality State: Essays on Intolerance and Inequality in Wyoming*. Western History Publications, 1999.

Madison, James. *The Writings of James Madison*. ed. Gaillard Hunt. New York: G.P. Putnam's Sons, 1900. Vol. 5. https://oll.libertyfund.org/titles/1937.

---. *Remembering Heart Mountain: Essays on Japanese American Internment in Wyoming*. Western History Publications, 1998.

Mihara, Sam. *The Life and Times of Sam Mihara: As Told to Alexandra Villarreal.* 2nd ed., Mihara Associates, 2019.

Mill, John Stuart. *On Liberty.* 1859. Dover Publications, 2002.

Muller, Eric L. *American Inquisition: The Hunt for Japanese American Disloyalty in World War II.* U of North Carolina P, 2007.

---. *Free to Die for Their Country: The Story of the Japanese American Draft Resisters in World War II.* U of Chicago P, 2001.

Neary, Ben. "Wyoming Indians Question Conservative Law Firm's Motives in 5-Year Federal Vote Rights Case." *Casper Star-Tribune,* 2 Dec. 2010.

Nelson, Fern K. *This Was Jackson's Hole.* High Plains Press, 1994.

Parker, Kathleen. "Kathleen Parker on the Challenge of Civility." *Washington Post,* 15 Nov. 2009, http://www. washingtonpost.com/wp-dyn/content/article/2009/11/13/ AR2009111303329.html.

Peters, John Durham. *Courting the Abyss: Free Speech and the Liberal Tradition.* U of Chicago P, 2005.

Rea, Tom. "Right Choice, Wrong Reasons: Wyoming Women Win the Right to Vote." November 8, 2014. https://www. wyohistory.org/encyclopedia/right-choice-wrong-reasons-wyoming-women-win-right-vote/.

Rochman, Bonnie. "Cyberbullying? Homophobia? Tyler Clementi's Death Highlights Online Lawlessness." *Time Healthland,* 1 Oct. 2010, healthland.time. com/2010/10/01/cyberbullying-homophobia-tyler-clementis-death-highlights-online-lawlessness/.

Ruble, Marko. "Hamburgers in Jeffrey City." Course pack for POLS 4710-01: Wyoming's Political Identity, compiled by Peter K. Simpson, 2006, U of Wyoming.

Sandefer, Ryan. "Recreational Communities: Wyoming's Changing Tourist Industry." Course pack for POLS 4710-01: Wyoming's Political Identity, compiled by Peter K. Simpson, 2006, U of Wyoming.

"The Seneca Falls Declaration of Sentiments" Fordham University Internet History Sourcebook. https://sourcebooks.fordham.edu/mod/senecafalls.asp

Shapin, Steven. *A Social History of Truth: Civility and Science in Seventeenth-Century England.* U of Chicago P, 1995.

Shepard, Judy. *The Meaning of Matthew: My Son's Murder in Laramie and the World Transformed.* Hudson Street Press, 2009.

Shepherd, Ken. "37 Percent of Americans Can't Name Any of the Rights Guaranteed by First Amendment: Survey." The Washington Times, 13 Sep. 2007, www.washingtontimes.com/news/2017/sep/13/37-percent-of-americans-cant-name-any-of-the-right/.

Stegner, Wallace. *Where the Bluebird Sings to the Lemonade Springs: Living and Writing in the West.* Modern Library, 2002.

Taylor, Astra. *Democracy May Not Exist, but We'll Miss It When It's Gone.* Holt, 2020.

---. *Examined Life.* Zeitgeist Films, 2019.

---. *What is Democracy?* Zeitgeist Films, 2019.

Tecumseh. "Speech to the Osages" History is a Weapon. https://www.historyisaweapon.com/defcon1/tecumosages.html

Thoreau, Henry David. "Civil Disobedience." *Walden and Other Writings*, edited by William Rossi and Owen Thomas, 2nd ed., Modern Library, 1992, pp. 665-694.

Tocqueville, Alexis de. *Democracy in America*. 1835. Signet Classics, 2010.

Truth, Sojourner. "Ain't I a Woman?" Fordham University Internet History Sourcebooks. https://sourcebooks. fordham.edu/mod/sojtruth-woman.asp

Washington, George. *Rules of Civility & Decent Behaviour in Company and Conversation: A Book of Etiquette*. Beaver Press, 1971.

West, Elliott. *The Contested Plains: Indians, Goldseekers, and the Rush to Colorado*. U of Kansas P, 1998.

Williams, Terry Tempest. *The Open Space of Democracy*. Orion Society, 2004.

Wright, Will. *The Wild West: The Mythical Cowboy and Social Theory*. Sage Publishers, 2001.